Infected Love

Identifying and Eliminating Toxic Relationship Killers

BY DION BRINSON SR.

INFECTED LOVE by Dion Brinson Sr.
Published by Hobbs Ministries, Inc.
Hobbs Ministries Publishing/Empowering Everyday Women, Inc.
2316 Delaware Ave.
#134
Buffalo, NY 14216

All rights reserved. No part of this publication may be reproduced, distributed, or transmitted in any form or by any means, including photocopying, recording, or other electronic or mechanical methods, without the prior written permission of the publisher, except in the case of brief quotations embodied in critical reviews and certain other noncommercial uses permitted by copyright law.

Unless otherwise indicated, all Scripture quotations are from the Holy Bible, New International Version. Copyright © 1973, 1978, 1984, International Bible Society. Used by permission.

Scripture quotations marked NKJV are from the New King James Version of the Bible. Copyright © 1979, 1980, 1982, by Thomas Nelson, Inc. Used by permission.

Scripture quotations marked CEV are from the Contemporary English Version® of the Bible. Copyright © 1995 American Bible Society. Used by permission.

Cover design by Joseph Brinson III
Copyright © 2018 by Dion Brinson
All rights reserved worldwide.

Printed in the United States of America
First Printing, 2018
ISBN-13: 978-0-578-40394-6

I dedicate this book to you, my beautiful wife, Kimberly. You are my best friend and confidante. Thank you for letting me share my ideas with you in the middle of the night. Somehow, you never got tired of listening. You have believed in me throughout this entire process as I read my ideas from the book to you over and over again. I am grateful for your patience, understanding and encouragement. I am so blessed to have you in my life. I love you.

Contents

Foreword..

Introduction...

Chapter 1: Are You Masking Scars And Bruises? 1

Chapter 2: Symptom-free Doesn't Mean Problem-free............12

Chapter 3: Holding On To Offenses Is Dangerous...................20

Chapter 4: Eventually Symptoms Will Show Up......................28

Chapter 5: It Is Possible To Survive...38

Chapter 6: It's Treatment Time..48

Chapter 7: Ask The Tough Questions......................................59

Chapter 8: It's Not You. It's The Infection................................71

Chapter 9: Be Careful Who You Run To..................................82

Chapter 10: Don't Play The Comparison Game.......................88

Chapter 11: Follow Through 100

Chapter 12: Know When It's Over...110

Chapter 13: Teamwork Makes The Dream Work....................126

Acknowledgments..138

About the Author...140

Foreword

I was about 15 years old when I built up the courage to tell my childhood crush of two years I was crushing on him. Big mistake! He responded, "What kind: orange, grape or cherry?"

Perhaps that was his humorous personality shining through or a polite way of making light of the situation, and letting me down easy. Either way, his response crushed my spirit, my ego and my pride.

I'm sensitive, stupid!

I didn't say that, but that's how I felt. I was shy and quiet, so coming out of my comfort zone to express how I felt about someone took a lot. After mustering up the courage to do it, only to feel rejected in the end, was one of many experiences that stayed with me. It shaped how I viewed things, people and situations, as well as how I would react to them.

When I met my husband Dion, who is a handsome, charismatic, intelligent, friendly, go-getter, I never imagined that issues—big and small—from my past would impact our union. I was sure I had it together. I was saved, had a good job, house, car, education and I traveled. I was on my way somewhere! I expected only the best. Besides, Dion is a patient, God-fearing man of God. He is also my best friend. How could things not be blissful?

He won me over with his smooth talk, magical smile and vision for the future. Then I fell in love and married him. Our wedding day was amazing. It was the beginning of a lifetime together. Still today, we laugh every now and then when we think back on our reception. We recall what a gentleman had to say who wasn't a part of our event. He commented on how he thought Dion was my father! Perhaps my husband looked like he was full of wisdom, or maybe I was making him old already. Ha!

Seriously though, it wasn't until years into our marriage that I saw how my own internal struggles, tied to my previous hurts, led me to react and process things a certain way. Walls were up when I thought there weren't any. Old baggage and pain I had refused to deal with surfaced. Eventually, I recognized that, until I addressed what was eating away at me inside, I would never be complete or fully happy.

Now, don't get me wrong, there were hurts that we *both* had to deal with, but my job wasn't to point out his faults or hurts. My task was to find the root of *my* pain. What happened in my life that caused a wound? Why hadn't I gotten it checked out? Why did I allow a scab to cover the psychological and emotional injury, never realizing that each time that spot was nicked, bumped or hit, it still hurt?

My opportunity to get to the root of my hurt almost came too late. Infection had set in. It pains me to think that our God-ordained marriage that I desperately wanted to work could have been over.

It took effort and patience on both of our parts to work through the tough times; but by the grace of God, we made it. We are both better for having stuck it out and done the work.

When Dion told me God gave him a book to write on love, I was his cheerleader! I loved the idea of him being able to use his wisdom rooted in personal experiences to help others. Furthermore, love is something God has dealt with him about very often, which makes sense, because God *is* love. Aside from knowing Dion's pure heart and seeing how he loves me, his assignment was divinely confirmed. It is also reconfirmed daily when others constantly seek him out for advice and help.

Infected Love is not for one specific group. Whether you're single or married, this book will help you. It is for everyone: those who are broken; those who are confused; those who fear it might be over for them; those who believe their time for love has passed; those who think that happiness eludes them; and those who always seem to be going in circles or cycles. I pray that you will ask God to open your eyes, ears and heart to receive the message in *Infected Love*, and that you will acknowledge any issues without fear.

Though the process may not be easy, it is definitely worth it. I know firsthand.

Kimberly Brinson

Wife of Dion Brinson

Introduction

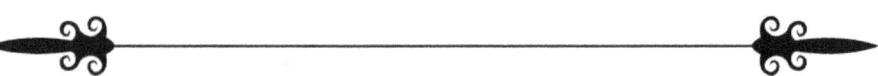

In the winter of 1918, near the end of World War I, an absolutely devastating influenza virus caused one of the deadliest epidemics in history. This is according to the U.S. Department of Health and Human Services.

The viral infection got so bad, businesses closed down, entire families died, buildings and homes had to be quarantined. By the summer of 1919, 675,000 Americans and 20 million people worldwide had died.

This is one of the scariest examples of the traumatizing impact an infection can have on mankind. Thankfully, today, there are effective flu vaccines, and incidents of death from influenza are less common. Still, nobody wants the flu. In fact, no one wants to get an infection at all.

An infection occurs when a virus, bacteria, parasite or some other disease-causing agent invades the body. It produces toxins that multiply and result in illness, pain and sometimes, even death. That's why, in *Infected Love*, I stress over and over again, when you feel like something is wrong, get it checked out. Waiting too long can be devastating to your relationship.

I have, in the past, avoided regular checkups. It's not that I feel invincible or that I don't care about my health. So what is it? Well, the thought of what *could* be wrong or what bad report the physician *might* give keeps me from making an appointment.

Have you ever had times when you absolutely knew you needed to be seen by a physician but avoided going anyway? Can you relate to this scenario? All the signs were there. You had strange aches, pains and sensations. You were fully aware that something was off with your body.

Yet, because of your nervousness about what may be revealed, you found every reason to overlook the negative symptoms. That is, until they become almost unbearable. Eventually, whether you wanted to or not, you had to break down and get to the doctor.

I have done that. And although it is not wise to let things get out of hand, we tend to do this with our natural health and in our relationships. When we don't address issues, however, they become like bacteria and multiply.

As more problems develop, our infection worsens and turns our love into toxic poison. Toxins kill off relationships, leaving us sad, angry and full of bitterness. If you don't want to see this happen in your life and relationship, it is necessary to put special measures in place to fight against infection. That is what *Infected Love* will help you do.

Whether you're in a healthy or harmful relationship, or are single and seeking out great relationship advice, this book will be beneficial in many ways. *Infected Love* will teach you how to identify hidden issues, zone in on symptoms that serve as warning signs of trouble ahead, and annihilate the infection that threatens the health of your love life.

Be warned: if you are looking for a way to point fingers at others, while ignoring your own toxicity, close the book. *Infected Love: Identifying and Eliminating Toxic Relationship Killers* is not for you.

But if you are prepared to target personal issues festering inside *your* heart, that are keeping you from experiencing a vibrant, fulfilling relationship, continue moving forward through these chapters.

As you read, you will understand why strong love is not enough to hold a relationship together if it is infected. An infection left untreated will surely cause the death of love, no matter how much you want to keep that relationship alive.

If you believe in your heart that love is worth fighting for and you are willing to take a hard look at yourself, this will be a life-changing book for you.

Before we get started, keep in mind that there are four stages of infection:

1) Incubation

2) Prodromal

3) Invasive

4) Convalescent

I will break down each stage throughout the book and give

you practical tips to apply in a series of short chapters. That way, you can immediately use the tools and techniques presented here to improve your relationship.

Though *Infected Love* is a quick read, don't just rapidly skim the pages without meditating on the principles and advice given. If you give focused attention to what's on each page, it will be well worth the time spent.

CHAPTER 1
Are You Masking Scars and Bruises?

There are some scars you and I have, but we don't remember how they got there. The scar, however, is evidence that something did, in fact, happen.

I have a scar on the right side of my cheek and it can only be seen when someone is paying close attention. My wife asked me one day, "What happened to your face?" I told her the story my mother told me.

Mom said, as a boy, every day I would watch my dad shave. One day, I went to the bathroom and got the bright idea to grab his razor and try to shave myself. Well, I wasn't quite ready yet. I cut myself pretty good in the process and thus, the remaining scar.

Even though I don't remember what happened, I have the mark—and Mom's retelling of the story— to prove there was an injury. Many of us are walking around with scars, both mentally and emotionally.

We don't even realize what happened to us or when it occurred. But, before we can love in a healthy manner, we must do some soul-searching and honest self-evaluating. Otherwise, we will forge relationships that will ultimately fail because we are out of touch with how our history affects our present.

When we have scars that impact our love, but don't remember what caused the injury, we can't fix things. If we try to give love away without dealing with our own inner-being, we'll spread toxic, tainted love unintentionally.

The Greatest Love

Love is the deepest emotion of the soul. It is so powerful that it allows people to overlook glaring imperfections. Through eyes of love, they are able to see past shortcomings and discover the most beautiful, perfect parts of someone, despite their faults.

The Bible shows us the greatest picture of love. As Romans 5:8 NLT says, "But God demonstrates his own love for us in this: While we were still sinners, Christ died for us." Now *that's* what it truly means to look past imperfections. Ponder the fact that when we were yet sinners Christ died for us. Amazing!

We were not perfect, but yet, He gave his life for us because of His unfailing and unconditional love. If we are to love like Christ, we must be willing to extend that same grace.

So ask yourself: *am I willing to love sacrificially? Am I committed to investing in my relationship and developing a bond that will last a lifetime? Am I serious about giving the greatest love, which is the selfless kind?*

I'll admit, that's easier said than done. In fact, it's impossible if your love is infected. Even in the healthiest relationships, love can be complicated. There are moments of happiness and joy. There are also moments of pain and suffering. Everyone has ups and downs. Though painful seasons aren't easy to cope with, after we get past them, they create the glue that develops a strong bond that can't be broken. Love that has been tried and tested is stronger than any other.

The average everyday ups and downs are normal. The drama associated with infected love is not. If an infection is present, things are overly complicated, mentally exhausting, emotionally draining and psychologically taxing. The union feels forced, difficult, joyless and impossible to endure. No couple wants these descriptions attached to their relationship. So then, how can this be avoided?

Start by identifying what love means to you and the person with whom you're sharing it. How do you view love? If you fail to define what love is for you and your significant other, you will fail in your relationship. We must know specifically what has molded and shaped our interpretation of love.

What were we exposed to growing up? Was there dysfunction in the models put before us? How did we develop our perceptions? Do we have healthy, balanced perspectives or extreme views? These are the kinds of things we must examine before we can know whether or not our love is healthy or infected.

Are you Scarred or Bruised?

A scar, by definition, is a mark left by the healing of a wound. For our purposes, it is evidence of a past emotional injury stemming from a painful experience. A scar could be the result of a divorce, rape, molestation or abuse of any kind.

Aside from scars, there are bruises, which many of us have also. You may ask, *what is the difference?* Well, bruising is an injury to the tissue without laceration to the skin. In most cases, bruises don't require a band aid. They cause discoloration to the skin that eventually disappears. Since an internal bruise does not leave a surface-level scar or cause external bleeding, it may not seem as serious.

But that isn't necessarily true. It all depends on the force of the impact. A boxer that has his ribs broken in a fight from a punch to the body does not show signs of a scar or bruise at that moment. Despite no evidence showing up right away, he is still fighting with broken bones.

Say a child hits her head very hard on the ground and

develops a bruise. Her parent knows not to let her go to sleep because of the potential damage. Though there is only a bruise present, it should not be dismissed; the damage has been done on the inside.

In life, emotional bruising isn't immediately visible outwardly, but it does instant damage inwardly. It destroys self-confidence and creates intimidation. It alters your personality and dissolves your happiness, replacing it with depression. If we are not careful, it can become detrimental to our lives.

Are you Masquerading?

There are many folks walking around bruised with a smile. Their happy demeanor doesn't mean *they* are happy. They could feel really stuck in a bad place, as if they are trapped and hopeless with no way out. They are bruised internally with a façade of contentment externally.

Has your smile become part of your masquerade? Are you empty, depleted and worn out without a sense of direction? Are you bruised inwardly while working hard not to let people see how tough the struggle really is within? You may look beautiful or handsome. You might seem to have it all together. Perhaps no one knows the real pain and hurt that torments your heart and mind every day.

You could be wounded inside hoping it will just get better on its own. It won't. You must stop masquerading, get in touch with what's really happening on the inside and get help.

If you have gone through a divorce or a bad breakup, that is enough to bruise you, though you may be unconscious of how deep the impact is. Without treatment, before you know it, you will shut out friends and loved ones.

Unknowingly, you will be deteriorating from the effects of your sorrow and pain. Guilt and self-blame will take over. You may feel like it was all your fault, as if you were the only one who caused the relationship to end. This may lead to feelings of being worthless, embarrassed and consumed by past failures in love.

Examine Yourself

Due to the fact that many of us haven't closely examined ourselves or our personal views on love, we have the wrong perception of what is going on in our hearts, minds and relationships. We're out of touch.

In the introduction of *Infected Love*, I talked about how some of us avoid going to the doctor's office. We ignore our pain and flare-ups to our own detriment. The same is true of our behaviors in everyday life. We get hurt. We feel pain. Still, we ignore it. This is a bad habit, because if there is a serious issue, not acknowledging it doesn't make it go away.

It makes it get worse—a point you will see me drive home

over and over again as you read. When we are too consumed with pouring ourselves into our relationship, or even trying to feed or repair someone else's emotions, we neglect ourselves. That's not good because obsessing over what someone else needs, means ignoring your own needs.

Examine yourself. If you don't, you'll never dig deep enough to identify the things that happened to *you* that have scarred you. You'll also overlook the factors that are presently impacting the health of your relationship. So don't skip over the personal examination and assessment phase.

You need to know all the things that shape your point of view on love. Analyze the driving factors behind your behaviors. This will help you out a lot when building up your relationship.

Do the work. Dig for clues. Find the answers. It's the key to saving your marriage or a relationship that is potentially leading to marriage.

Before you move on to the next chapter:

Grab a journal or notebook. You will need it throughout the book to jot down your thoughts, feelings, questions and answers. In it, write about the models of love you saw growing up.

- Did you see healthy marriages?
- Divorces?
- Abuse?
- Also, write down at least one past relationship or experience that was painful for you that still affects you in some way today.

CHAPTER 2

Symptom-free Doesn't Mean Problem-free

The first phase of infection is Incubation. The incubation period is the amount of time between you catching an infection and symptoms actually showing up. You can be infected and show no signs at all.

When I was a teenager, I remember getting Chicken Pox. I had a fever. I was achy and covered in itchy blisters. One of my younger sisters was fascinated with the Chicken Pox and for some reason, she wanted to see if she could actually catch them from touching a blister.

She had heard they were highly contagious but was skeptical, so she put everyone's word to the test. For days, after touching a blister, nothing happened. More than a week passed and still nothing showed up on her skin.

What she didn't know is that the incubation period for Chicken Pox is between 14-16 days. The infectious virus can be in your body for over two weeks with no symptoms. One day, my younger sibling noticed a small bump on her stomach. Since it was only one and wasn't too itchy, she thought nothing of it. That was all about to change.

After five days passed, that one bump turned into multiple. Next thing she knew, she was feverish, aching, itching and covered in a blister-like rash. She didn't believe she was infected until the signs were obvious. But her immune system had already been compromised before the first bump showed up.

Our body has built-in mechanisms to fight germs and bacteria, so symptoms can be held off for a while. But when there are too many invaders, because our system can only handle so much, after a while our immune system breaks down. It gives over to the attack. That's when we get noticeably ill.

Each of us, at some point, has come into contact with an infection that's still in the incubation stage. We can contract it through unexpected and unsuspected ways. It can get in through an open wound that has not been cared for properly.

For example, when we get a cut, we wash the cut and apply antiseptic immediately, along with a bandage, right? We take these precautions so that infection does not get in through the exposed wound.

But things get a whole lot trickier when it comes to our heart being wounded. We can't see that type of injury. We might think we're perfectly okay since what's wrong isn't visible to the natural eye.

So we go through an incubation period where the internal bleeding goes undetected. It's not until we exhibit signs of toxic behaviors that it becomes obvious that there's something going on within. Have you ever seen someone fall down hard or get into a bad accident? You and others rush to their assistance because they are visibly injured. Obvious wounds make us respond. We tend to take some sort of action.

But what do you do when your wounds are private? How do you handle internal bleeding and deeply personal pain? Who is going to bandage an invisible wound?

Often, in life and love, when you fall or get knocked down through some kind of hurt, there is no help for you. Unfortunately, that neglect makes it easier for your love to become infected. With no first aid, the wound doesn't heal properly. Bacteria gets in. Still, it is ignored until there is an outbreak of negativity and toxicity that can no longer be overlooked.

Communicate, Don't Incubate.

What happens when someone is afraid to communicate their pain or refuses to do so because they do not know how to articulate their emotions? They employ a form of deliberate incubation.

That means they purposely hide or conceal their issues. They bottle their feelings up and try to handle everything on their own. But that's a huge mistake. Eventually, what's under the surface will rise to the top.

Let me interject something about communication here: it is a two-way connection. On both ends there is a receiver, meaning each person should listen. Some of us seem to be unaware of this. So we walk around with a bullhorn, blurting out all of our emotions, but never giving our partner an opportunity to speak.

Constantly overpowering the one that's listening, without giving them a chance to respond, will only cause feelings of neglect and hurt. This leaves the person on the other side of that bullhorn with an open wound in their heart because they never got to share their feelings.

Communication is a challenge in many relationships and this problem needs immediate attention. Failing to resolve this will be disastrous. To illustrate this point, let's focus on the hen. It sits on its eggs through the incubation phase. This kind of hen is called a "broody."

The broody uses the warmth of its body to set the right temperature and conditions for the chicken to grow. For 21 days the hen sits on the egg. Then it hatches and out pops a chicken. If you are trying to hatch chickens, brooding is a good thing. But in relationships, being a broody that sits on issues doesn't help anything. It only serves to delay the inevitable. The issues, like an egg after 21 days of incubation, will hatch. They will pop out. Someone is going to explode.

Are you the broody in your relationship? Have you been hurt by someone and haven't dealt fully with that offense? If so, it's not healthy to incubate the egg, which is a metaphor for an uncommunicated issue. It's not smart to sit on issues; it's only a matter of time before they hatch, crack through the fragile outer shell and come bursting out into the open. Communicate, don't incubate.

Have you ever heard someone say *the squeaky wheel gets the oil* or *closed mouths don't get fed?* The idea is that those who verbalize their needs are more likely to get them met. There's no way anyone can address what is broken, hurting and wounded in you if you won't articulate your issues. You don't have to be eloquent. Just do your best to say what you need.

Before you move on to the next chapter:

Get honest about some issues you may be holding on to that you need to open up about.

- Write about them in your journal. This will help you identify what resentment you may be harboring.

- At the appropriate time, if you are in a relationship, share these things with your partner. It's the only way to take real steps toward working through the problems poisoning your relationship.

CHAPTER 3

Holding On To Offenses Is Dangerous

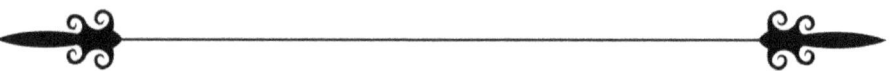

When I lived at home with my parents, they had one of those old school pressure cookers. At the top of it was a release valve. When too much steam built up inside, you had to turn the release valve and let the pressure cooker blow out some steam.

Well, one day, they waited too long to turn the release valve. The pressure built up so much until it wound up blowing the lid off, hitting the ceiling and splattering the contents of the pot all over the kitchen. It was literally a hot mess!

If you want to make a hot mess of your relationship, all you have to do is incubate your issues instead of dealing with them. One day, when the pressure gets to be too much, you will blow your top. If you feel mistreated, communicate that; don't incubate it. Otherwise, you will hit the ceiling and your partner will be thinking, *why didn't you tell me anything was wrong?*

Are you Incubating Offenses?

Without communicating, our hearts become an incubator for offenses. When someone offends you that means what they did caused you to feel violated in some way. As a result, you get upset, annoyed or resentful. This can turn your love toxic if it's not dealt with in a timely manner.

Think about how the incubator works in the case of a premature baby. This special chamber controls the infant's temperature and protects them from infections. They are safe inside the incubator until they grow healthy and strong enough to function outside of this clear, crib-sized dome.

As we have established, in relationships, if you incubate negative things, like a premature baby, they will grow stronger. If you hold grudges instead of talking about what's bothering you, you're incubating offense. It will grow from the size of a molehill into a huge mountain your partner cannot climb over.

Do you realize that you become an incubator for infection when you get tight-lipped about what is vexing you instead of opening up? You make the toxic situation far worse. You deepen your own sorrow and blow things way out of proportion when you hold on to all that hostility. Why keep it in? Turn that pressure release valve before it's too late.

As you read, do a self-evaluation. Are you incubating offenses by harboring ill feelings? Maybe deep down you think your spouse doesn't appreciate you. You may have cleaned the entire house, cooked dinner and kept the kids quiet so he could get some rest for work, and he didn't show any signs of gratefulness. Maybe he didn't tell you how beautiful you looked after you got dressed just for him.

Perhaps she didn't show appreciation for that gesture of kindness you went out of your way to make. It could be that she didn't have dinner ready all week when you came home after completing your 12-hour shift from work.

You could be upset that he spent more nights out at the office, events, or with friends than he did with you. You could be annoyed that they seem more concerned about their selfish desires than making the relationship a happy one. Offenses within relationships can stem from many things. They are unavoidable, but communication about them should *never* be avoided.

Relationship Poison

Uncommunicated and unresolved offenses are relationship poison. Here's an example of why. Let's say you enjoyed the smile, compliment, or look someone gave you while passing by earlier that day. That gesture could be innocent.

But if you feel like *they* are giving you the kind of attention you aren't getting at home, you could nurse that thought-seed and have it blossom into something unhealthy.

Instead of finding ways to feed your starving emotional needs at home, you start saying things like, *if they don't quit tripping, I can have someone else*—like that person who smiled and flirted. So then you walk through the front door of your house with a cold, entitled and distant attitude, already pondering how to have your void filled elsewhere.

You stop putting in the effort in your relationship. You are consumed with what you are lacking in your life, and become willing to entertain other options for your own satisfaction. If resentment has been festering and incubating, it will affect how you interpret and react to what you have seen or heard from a third party.

Let go of poisonous offenses. They will ruin something that could be saved, worked on, fixed and nurtured. Everyone feels upset and slighted at times. No one is perfect and there isn't a person on earth that gets it right one hundred percent of the time. But if you let that seed of offense be planted, watered and nurtured, it will grow. And like weeds in a garden, it will choke out all the good stuff.

What Kind of Environment are You Creating?

We have been dealing extensively with how relationships can be easily undermined in the incubation phase. I have been stressing that whatever the origin of the dissatisfaction, disappointment or hurt is, it has to be dealt with before it fully develops into something dangerous.

To recap, the incubator is your heart. The infection is the unresolved issue. The only way the infection can survive is if you provide the right environment for it to thrive. You do that by nursing hurt instead of communicating about what's going on within you. If you, like a hen, continue brooding and sitting on that issue, your situation will eventually hatch into a major problem.

A woman who feels neglected by her spouse in the area of intimacy, or feels ignored emotionally, becomes wounded. If she is not careful, she will hold on to resentment and hostility, and infection can set in. It starts in the environment of the mind and emotions. Negative thoughts run wild.

Unchecked emotions go crazy. Feelings of being ignored and deep longing for attention turn into bitterness and dissatisfaction. Bruised feelings and stored up offenses, like bacteria, can quickly multiply, spread, and become a full-blown infection.

> *Before you move on to the next chapter:*
>
> Pull out your journal once again.
>
> - Think about the ways you create an environment for infection to grow. Write about it.
> - For example, you may write, *I avoid issues, so they grow bigger.* By being candid and real, you can recognize unhealthy patterns and do better going forward.

CHAPTER 4
Eventually Symptoms Will Show Up

Growing up, I was one of 14 siblings. There were 3 older than me and 10 younger. There was always a lot of excitement when we were together. So many of my brothers and sisters are talented, especially in the areas of singing and playing instruments.

At any given time we would have church in the living room or a concert in the kitchen. We laughed so much. It was awesome. My mother and father were wonderful parents. Dad believed in eating together at dinnertime—something I practice to this day. Even though the bond of our family was strengthened around the dinner table, preparing a meal daily for a family of our size was quite the task. Feeding us required lots of groceries and time.

Whoever prepared the food needed plenty of patience. But, despite the level of sacrifice, I never heard my mother or father say *I am tired of cooking for you!* They didn't ever seem impatient with the process. But me? I didn't have patience. I would start asking, *what's for dinner?* Then, no sooner than I'd walked out of the kitchen, I would come right back and ask, *how long is it going to take?* After a while, my dad would say, "Boy, go sit down and wait!"

Needless to say, I didn't ask any more questions after that. While not-so-patiently waiting, I would hear the chicken frying on the stove. The oven would open and shut, and the aroma would smell so good I could almost pass out from anticipation. Then Mom or Dad would finally shout, "Come and eat!"

There would be so much food to consume, especially on holidays. We would all fix our plates, sit at the table and wait for the blessing before we could dig in. As you can imagine, there was a lot of waiting with such a large family.

But after each scrumptious meal was over, I never thought about how long I had to wait. I ate and was satisfied, and only remembered how good the food was, not the extended time period it took to get it.

Like preparing a good meal for a large family, creating the environment for a healthy, positive relationship requires lots of patience and work. It doesn't happen overnight; nor does resentment, deep-rooted bitterness, seething anger and cold-heartedness vanish overnight.

Resentment builds over time. And then, the symptoms of what's been cooking over weeks, months and sometimes years of incubation, manifests.

Infection is Contagious

When someone is infected in a relationship, that infection is contagious. It impacts both them and their partner. It is transmitted through words and deeds. These become *fomites*, which is a term for objects or materials that are likely to carry infection.

Clothes, utensils, and furniture are the perfect fomites because infection is transmitted from surfaces and even other people. In relationships, if only one partner is infected, because infection is contagious, over time, both parties will be affected.

Negative symptoms will show up in the form of mood swings, distance, snappiness, disrespect, crying, sadness, irritability, quick-temperedness, blame, depression, eating disorders, and even violent outbursts. The negative buildup of emotion is a direct result of a wound, or several wounds, not being properly cared for in the beginning. Getting things taken care of and treated as soon as possible is critical.

Let's consider a man who does not receive honor in his own home. Say he is disrespected and overlooked. Since being vulnerable is hard for him, he doesn't express what he truly feels. He won't tell you that a man operates off of his ego and there is a need for him to feel needed.

After all, many men don't know how to articulate their feelings or they are too stubborn to make the attempt. This leaves space for infection to set in. He holds on to that hurt in silence.

In the incubation phase, despite there being a problem, there are no real symptoms yet. Once the effects show up—and they inevitably will— the disgruntled man becomes aware of his feelings of humiliation, emasculation, rejection and betrayal. He feels the pain that can range from mild aches, to localized discomfort, all the way to unbearable agony.

When he hurts, his partner winds up hurting, too. That

infection is passed along as hostility, brazenness and what seems like loss of interest. No one wants that to happen.

Get Real

How can you keep negative symptoms at bay? You do that by getting real with yourself. What has hurt you? Identify it, but don't incubate it. Talk about it. Get rid of those negative emotions. Don't let them remain trapped inside or they will cause your love to be infected.

As you have already learned, the first stage of infection is the incubation phase. A quick refresher: this is the time between when the infection enters the body and the appearance of its first symptom. It can start out as loneliness and longing to be with someone. If that emptiness and yearning remains unaddressed, any type of conversation or attention will do—no matter *who* it comes from. You'll find yourself looking for something or anyone to satisfy that craving of the soul. Don't let things go that far. Don't neglect each other in the area of intimacy. Refusing sex is harmful to a marriage. However, what is even more damaging, is not communicating with each other, so talk through it.

Get real. You can resolve many things if you just open up. You can do it. Try it. Discuss the issues. But whatever you do, don't incubate them. They'll only turn into a bunch of negative symptoms and highly contagious problems.

Drop your Defenses

Shutting down is a defense mechanism for men and some women. But let me deal specifically with the brothers. Despite evidence showing up in our love life that things need to be addressed, we often refuse to do so in a fruitless effort to protect our minds, emotions and ultimately, our hearts.

So many times we ignore what we could do to make

something better, not only because of fear, but also, because of pride. We wonder how we will be perceived and received. Our egos frequently get in the way of what we know we should be doing.

But putting defenses and walls up doesn't help. It creates more problems and symptoms that will be harder to get rid of later. Medically speaking, infections worsen with time and are tougher to treat. Relationally speaking, infections get worse with time also, and are tougher to treat. You can't win with defensiveness and neglectfulness. Drop the walls. Address the issues.

For men, this idea of vulnerability can be a very scary thing. Men don't often give their hearts away. We don't like letting our guard down, so we seldom act on emotions of the heart. Putting up a façade and holding things inside gives tainted thoughts and feelings a place to dwell and grow.

Our love gets infected by a mixture of pride and fear, which undermines what could be healthy love. Our defenses alter the way we respond physically and emotionally. It reduces our level of engagement in the relationship. We get distant. A man can be in love, but too infected to show it. It is a sad state to be in, although millions suffer from this syndrome.

If you are experiencing this, do something about it. Now that you see the symptoms showing up, address these issues. The infection won't go away on its own. Being less defensive is a choice. So choose to drop those defenses in order to promote healing and reconciliation.

Before you move on to the next chapter:

What symptoms, if any, are you noticing in yourself? Don't worry about your partner for now. Focus on you.

- Are you distant? Angry? Insensitive? Cold-hearted? Uninterested in sex? Short-tempered?

- Write your symptoms down below and try to identify the root cause of that infection.

My Worst Symptoms that Must Be Addressed:

_____

_____

_____

_____

_____

Now you can move on to the next chapter with full awareness of what you're truly dealing with. No matter how dire your symptoms are, you can recover if you're willing to do the work.

CHAPTER 5
It Is Possible To Survive

Symptoms don't mean death unless you're already too weak and damaged to ward off infection. Every marriage does not have to end in divorce. It is possible to survive hardship, tragedy and problems.

Just because something has scarred you emotionally does not mean that you cannot overcome it and eventually live in freedom. But you have to make sure you're constantly working on the relationship. Strengthen your bond. That way, if the infection does temporarily cause issues, they won't last. You'll be strong enough to fight the infection and regain total health.

If you are already weak, struggling and barely getting by, that complicates things drastically. If you have been incubating that infection, you have made it hard to treat and get rid of. Therefore, the demise of your relationship is more likely. Don't let that happen. When symptoms show up, move immediately toward resolving any issues. Early intervention is prevention against a failed relationship. You can survive this.

In chapter one, do you remember when we discussed emotional bruises? If not cared for properly, they will eventually expose themselves in your romantic relationship, friendship, parenting and life in general. That is why you have to deal with whatever caused those wounds.

Imagine if my mother didn't take care of the cut from the razor I mentioned previously. Can you guess what might have happened? Infection may have set in and caused my scar to be more pronounced today. Because of the care that was given, it's not as noticeable unless someone is standing very close.

Your Scar is Showing

When you get into a serious relationship, those closest to you can see your scars. They can tell that something happened to you to make you the way you are. They may not know the backstory, but they know something's not right.

In order to minimize the negative impact of a wound on your relationship, treating it, paying attention to it and nursing it is a must. It takes work, focus and determination to make sure you are healthy so your relationship will also be healthy.

Growing up, do you recall seeing people that were in what

seemed like good relationships? Didn't that make you desire to have the same thing?

Looking from the outside in, that model couple seemed nearly perfect, didn't they? But we don't know what it took to get there, do we? We don't know the work they put in. We have no insight into the obstacles they had to overcome or how hard they had to fight to make their relationship strong.

Yet, even without knowing all their relationship entailed, the picture of romance they presented was enough to inspire us to eventually take a chance with our hearts. But then we came face-to-face with the reality that things don't always go according to our plan. Relationships, on occasion, can go haywire and make love seem like an unattainable, unrealistic, idealistic, crazy idea.

But love isn't crazy. The real kind, despite bumps in the road, is forgiving, giving, patient, understanding and caring. It is not judgmental or partial and it does not cost anything. It's free.

Love is special. It's beautiful. We all want to experience it. So we must do whatever we need to do to cultivate and grow it.

Today, if your scars are showing, don't hide them. Don't pretend they aren't there. Examine the backstory. Be honest about what caused those emotional scars. Get real about the bruising or baggage, and get down to the business of dealing with it. It's all about caring for and treating our wounds by doing the internal work necessary to be whole. If you're serious about survival, get to work.

A Prayer for You

Help me God I'm sinking,

Life has passed by so fast without me blinking,

Being engulfed by my heart of pain has me unconsciously thinking,

About all the dreams I've been dreaming,

Snuffed out by the past hurts that are still lingering,

Smacked so hard by guilt and shame my ears are still ringing,

Help me God I'm sinking,

I don't want this to be my story's ending.

Silent Wounds

We have already established that there are some hurts that show no visible wounds initially. They can be compared to whiplash. Whiplash is a neck injury that happens due to force of impact. It is typically caused by a car accident, but can also be the result of any kind of blow that causes your neck to jerk forward too hard or fast.

The muscles and ligaments in your neck stretch too far and tear, causing painful muscle strain. Whiplash is particularly brutal because you get hit by something you never saw coming.
Most times, there are no side effects of the muscle injury until later.

In fact, some of us are walking around with whiplash of the heart. Let's explore this idea further.

Someone comes along and everything is wonderful. It feels like taking a new car out on a nice Sunday drive. Nothing seems to compare to the excitement and newness of the relationship. All is well and you are still trying to figure out exactly who this beautiful person is that you have met. In the beginning stages you think they are everything you prayed for.

The exterior is nice to look at. They are polite and respectful. They have many kind words to say that make your heart leap. When you are together it feels like only the two of you exist in this great big world. Both of you share the same interests. It all seems perfect. You begin to open up and give them your heart and mind. In some cases, your body, too.

Then, one day, the calls stop. No reply to your text messages. Everything ceases with no explanation. Boom!

Whiplash. It feels like an accident you never saw coming. You become someone who leaves the scene of a vehicle collision without an ambulance. You feel okay at that moment. You feel that you don't need to see a doctor. Without being aware of it, you leave with a silent wound.

You never saw the divorce, separation, abuse or rape coming and now the way you love has been infected. It is not until a bit of time passes that you feel the effects of what happened.

Suddenly, the stiff neck, back pain and headaches start. What if someone asked, *why didn't you go see the doctor?* You'd probably say, *I didn't know I was hurt.* Now think back over your life.

Ponder these questions:

- What silent wounds have you sustained that you have not dealt with?
- What devastated you without warning?

- What left you with the effects of whiplash that didn't show up until you were involved with a new person?

- Has your love been infected by the crash of your previous relationship?

- Could it be that the breakup you went through had done damage that you didn't recognize at the time?

If you discovered the damage too late, the expression "tore up from the floor up" probably describes your life. It has become hard to keep it all together. You want to be loved but are too afraid to open your heart again.

You are not alone. This is what happens in many relationships when one or both parties sustained injuries previously. This is far more common than you might imagine. Past trauma has a way of locking us into a prison.

We feel trapped and doomed to serve out a life sentence behind the bars of guilt, shame, bitterness, unforgiveness and hopelessness. But there are keys to breaking free if you want to be whole. It starts with identifying your silent wounds.

Before you move on to the next chapter:

Write down some places in your life where you sustained silent wounds.

- Infidelity? Separation? Abandonment?
- Divorce?
- Domestic violence?
- Sexual assault?
- Sudden death of a partner? Verbal abuse?
- Identify what gave you "whiplash," so you can heal the tear in your heart.

CHAPTER 6

It's Treatment Time

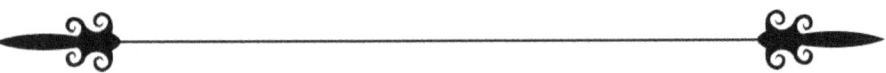

No more ignoring the issues. No more avoiding tough questions. No more blocking painful memories. The moment of reckoning has come.

First, ask yourself, *why didn't I go to the doctor? Why didn't I get treated?* In keeping with the car wreck analogy, you saw the car was mangled when you walked away. The emergency responders were only able to rescue you by cutting you out of the vehicle. You even said to yourself, *I don't know how I made it.* But just because you are able to walk away does not mean that you are okay.

The emotional whiplash I talked about in chapter 5 is unpleasant. It results from experiences and situations that were so devastating it seemed like you wouldn't survive. But you did. The painful side effects, however, are delayed in their manifestation. But there is something very important for you to remember.

Just because you survived the experience does not mean you are in the best condition to live afterwards. I'm not talking about existing, but rather, *living in freedom.* Sure, you got out with your life. Your heart is yet beating. You're still here. But are you alive? Are you thriving? Are you whole?

You can't truthfully say yes to that without getting the

proper help. It's time to get treated. Why haven't you taken any real steps to get better? Is it because the painful incident is too traumatizing to revisit? Is it that you assume time will repair the damage? It won't.

You must deal with the shock and resulting pain from it. If you have experienced emotional whiplash, your life has been shaken up. Realize that you need to recover. You got hit without having an opportunity to adequately brace for it. Something rocked your world. You lost something vital and precious, and it left you in pieces.

Stolen

It was all stolen,

My love, my marriage, my innocence,

And it left my heart broken.

I didn't ask for this.

Abundance, good health, a wonderful marriage,

That was my promise.

So now what do I do?

What about loyalty, faith and God?

Really this has me all confused.

I was loving and sincere and always focused,

Now I am hurt and ashamed

Why me? I don't deserve this.

Lord, please help me because I feel like my life is on pause,

better yet frozen,

I have been crushed to pieces because my life has been stolen.

Don't Pretend It Doesn't Hurt

Have you ever seen a young kid with a tough exterior pretending not to be hurt after a fall or some other physical blow?

"So what, it didn't hurt," they say, jumping up and pretending to immediately recover. Everyone laughs but they continue to insist, "I barely even felt it." Oh, but they felt it alright.

If you looked deep into their eyes in those moments and studied their facial expressions, you would have seen that just beneath the surface, they were about to crack. Their lips slightly quivered.

Their eyes filled with tears. They unconsciously placed their hand over the wound, nursing the pain. Their words betrayed their true feelings. They walked away with a skinned knee and a limp; a bruised arm and a cut; a wounded ego and lots of pretense.

As adults, unfortunately, in relationships, we have this tendency, too. We fall down and hurt ourselves, but don't want the embarrassment of anyone knowing we're hurt.

"So what, it didn't hurt," we say, jumping up and pretending to immediately recover. But that's not healthy. If something has been stolen, lost or stripped away from you, it hurts. Admit it. Don't pretend like it did not affect you. Don't just walk away rubbing on the wound and presuming that you don't need help. You need first aid. You need to be healed, because what you don't address today will resurface tomorrow. That wound will become infected and that's where the real problems begin.

Don't struggle in silence. Don't walk away like nothing ever happened. Something *did* happen. It impacted your psyche and your emotions. It broke you down. But that's okay. It happens to all of us at some point. But with time and the proper care, you can be whole again. It's time to be treated.

Pretending like you're not hurting may make you look strong outwardly for a moment. But the truth of the matter is, without treating the issues, you're getting weaker by the day and weakness is dangerous. Crying because you're hurting is not weakness.

Admitting you need help coping and getting through devastation is not weakness. Weakness is faking strength while you know, deep inside, you're in critical condition.

Infection attacks what is weak. Just like the flu can more easily kill a young child or an elderly person because their immune system is weaker, issues more easily kill off weaker relationships.

When you don't deal with your issues, this makes you and your relationship more susceptible to attacks. What wouldn't ordinarily cause fatality will take a struggling relationship out.

When you sustain a wound and you don't bandage yourself up, you leave yourself open. This makes you vulnerable. It lets more germs infiltrate and cause you greater harm. You get infected. The question then becomes, *how can you stop the infection right now at this early stage?*

Perhaps your relationship hasn't gotten to a more advanced stage of infection and you want to do everything to prevent it from getting there. It starts with you being honest with yourself. You must do a self-check.

Many times we hate to get real with ourselves, because it causes us to let down our guard emotionally. When we have been hurt, we tend to try to protect our hearts by erecting a wall. This defense mechanism, while very normal, at the same time, is very unhealthy.

Putting walls up hurts you the most. So instead of building a fortress around you, drop those defenses. Catch those issues early. In order to do that, you have to be honest with both yourself and your mate. Get to the root. Face the cold, raw, hard truth. It will make all the difference in your life.

To Listen is to Strengthen

If you want to catch a problem early and stop it from infecting and destroying your love, effective listening is important. Lots of people don't like to do it, but to listen is to strengthen your relationship.

You not only want to *hear* the person, but *try to get a real understanding* without pre-judging them. Remain open and do your part to help resolve the issue. Do your best to identify solutions that will benefit the relationship.

But here's a warning: in doing this, you must be careful not to be selfish, thinking only of your wants and needs. The focus can't be on you. It has to be on the growth and development of the relationship.

A big part of effective listening is knowing that you are not always right. Don't be overly-anxious to prove your point and win your partner over to your side. You must choose your battles wisely. It's okay to compromise.

Being flexible and willing to give in does not make you weak. It means you're mindful of how important finding that middle ground is. Now we're getting into the nuts and bolts of what it takes to save a relationship and get past the hurting part and on to the healing part.

Before you move on to the next chapter:

It's time to do some soul-searching and put your answers in your journal. Dig deep and ask yourself these questions:

- Do I love this person with all of my heart?
- Do I want to spend the rest of my life with him/her?
- Am I willing to do what it takes for us to make it in this relationship?
- Am I open to truly listening to the other person?

If your answer is *no* to most of the questions, be careful. That does not mean the union is definitely doomed. It simply means you have more work to do in order to have a successful relationship. Much communication is needed regarding why you feel this way. Tackle these underlying issues. It takes two to begin a relationship and it also takes two to improve one.

CHAPTER 7
Ask the Tough Questions

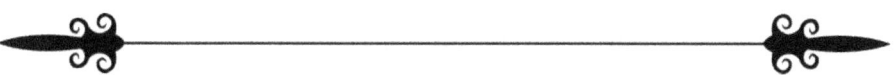

When I was a freshman at Buffalo State College, I had a part-time job at a restaurant to keep a little change in my pocket. At that time, one of my younger sisters, Dianna, was just entering her freshmen year at Bennett High School. I was so excited for her because she was growing up.

She walked to school every day and since I had to walk the

same way to catch the train, we strolled together. Each day we stopped at a doughnut shop in the Central Park Plaza called *Famous Doughnuts* to buy a bag of day-old doughnuts for 60 cents.

Sometimes the day-old doughnuts would be extra stale. But some days they'd taste freshly baked. We were always pleasantly surprised when that happened. On mornings when I didn't have enough change for our sugary breakfast, we would scavenge for coins just so we could buy the day-old doughnuts and munch on them together.

We didn't ask our parents for the money because this was a routine we created and shared together; that made it special and personal. I remember how cold and snowy the winters would be. The wind blew so hard, but that didn't bother us too much. We would still laugh and talk, get our doughnuts and then go our separate ways.

I enjoyed that semester of having the same schedule as Dianna. It felt like I got to know her for the first time. What makes this all so weird is that we lived in the same household all of our lives. Yet, somehow, we never really knew each other. I had 13 other siblings and 11 of them were at home back then.

Arguably, there wasn't much time to really sit down one-on-one and get to know each other. We all had a lot of fun together, though. We shared laughter and as much time together as we could.

But those morning walks with Dianna changed our relationship. I saw more of her individuality. I discovered what she liked and what some of her goals and aspirations were. Most of all, I realized that she really loved me as her big brother.

Though I don't live in Buffalo, New York anymore, every time I go back, I still visit *Famous Doughnuts*, now on Main Street.

I no longer have to buy the day-old doughnuts, thank God. But I do remember fondly my get-to-know-you sessions with Dianna all those years ago.

Isn't it amazing that we can live in the same house and be strangers? You can be in a relationship and under the same roof with a person and never truly get to know them. They may be called spouse, but that's just a label and doesn't necessarily indicate that there is a deep level of intimacy.

What Questions have you Asked?

Are you in a relationship with a stranger? Are there things you're overlooking and insights you're missing out on because you're not asking questions?

Think about when you visit the doctor's office. Before the physician or nurse prescribes a treatment, they listen, right? They ask questions: where does it hurt? How long has this been going on? What are your symptoms? How do you feel right now? Have you taken any medications or done anything to relieve the pain? How did those treatments work? Is there any history of specific types of diseases in your family?

The doctor investigates and listens before determining the right course of treatment. We have to do the same thing because it's ludicrous to try and treat symptoms we don't understand.

It's impossible to make someone happy in a marriage when you don't know who they are. Furthermore, a person can't satisfy your needs if they don't understand what those needs are.

If you have not yet married the person you're in love with, this is a good place to check your motives. What tough questions have you asked yourself?

Why do you believe that this is the right one?

Why would you marry them?

Is it based on the opinions of your family members?

Are you being pressured to jump the broom because of a pregnancy? Are you settling because your biological clock is ticking and you feel like you may as well walk down the aisle?

If you say "*I Do*" for the wrong reasons, that can leave you regretting what you have done. That's why this asking phase is crucial. Become like an investigative reporter. Make yourself the subject of the investigation. Don't assume you know things. Don't just look on the surface. Go deeper.

It's better to ask and answer these pressing questions now, rather than regretting your failure to do so later. If you have solid answers to your inquiries and feel confident moving forward in your relationship, then you have a great chance of starting a marriage out on a good foundation.

Don't Ignore These Signs

I was at home in bed when I received a call from my mother saying that she had taken my dad to the emergency room. She wanted me to come to the hospital. When I got there, I noticed some of my sisters gathered in the waiting room. They said Mom was with Dad.

When I located the area where my father was, my mother was standing next to his bed. I asked her what was wrong him. She said she was waiting on the doctor. All she knew was that Dad had a very high fever.

I remember him sitting up in bed trying to explain something to us, but we weren't able to understand him. What he was trying to articulate didn't come out in plain words. It was gibberish. I had never seen my father like this before.

His fever was so high that he seemed completely out of touch with reality. I watched my mom patiently try to decode the nonsensical words. After being given some medicine, Dad's fever began to lower and he was able to express his ideas much better.

I recall my father explaining how, before doctors administered the necessary medicines to clear up the infection, he couldn't communicate. He knew what he was *trying* to say, but when he opened his mouth the words would not come out the way he intended.

He said it was one of the most terrible and frustrating feelings he had ever experienced! The doctor came in and let us know that when someone's temperature gets too high, this can happen.

He also informed us that Dad's fever was because of an infection that had not yet been treated. Before physicians helped him, my father didn't know what was causing his symptoms. He was simply aware of the fact that he was not feeling well.

Pay Attention

Isn't it fascinating how an infection can be present without us knowing it's there? Not until the symptoms begin showing up do we have any inkling that something may be wrong.

I shared this story about my dad because, in many cases, our love has become infected and we don't understand exactly what's happening. All we know is that something has changed. Our mood is different. We no longer laugh and play. All the kind words we used to utter, we no longer say.

The times you couldn't wait to see one another are long gone. Intimacy becomes something you are no longer interested in. Pay attention when this happens. These symptoms are showing up because something is terribly wrong.

When you are symptomatic, you have entered the second stage of infection known as the *Prodromal Period*. In this phase, the number of infectious agents start increasing and the immune system begins reacting to them. Non-specific symptoms occur like fever, headaches, discomfort and lack of appetite.

At this point, wear and tear on your relationship becomes obvious, but it's not hopeless. Most of the time, in this stage, the infected person still loves their significant other, but can't explain what has happened. They will tell you they don't know why they feel this way and say phrases like, *we are just falling apart,* or *there is no spark there anymore*. Again, pay attention.

There has to be a reason why when you look at your mate you no longer feel the love you once had. Investigate. Ask questions. There is an underlying cause and you can find it. Why is it that the one who used to delight you now sickens you? What happened to the days when looking into their eyes would automatically cause you to daydream about the good times you've had or that you're *about* to have? What makes you burn up with anger when they talk to you?

These symptoms are telling you that the relationship is in an unhealthy state. There is an infection poisoning your once pure love. It's frustrating, I know. Communication isn't working. The words don't come out right. You feel that your partner is out of touch with reality and they may feel the same way about you. Temperatures rise, but not in a good way. Anger flares. What can you do?

Before you move on to the next chapter:

Get your journal and document your symptoms. Be specific.

- Are you angry? Sad? Disappointed? Ready to walk away?

- Get real about it, because if you don't, the symptoms will become deadly and ruin your relationship before you have a chance to treat what's wrong.

CHAPTER 8

It's Not You. It's the Infection.

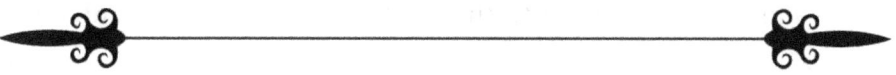

When I'm physically hurting and don't know why, I take whatever I can to eliminate the pain. Do you do that, too? I become my own doctor.

I'll be taking back pain medicine for my throat or Nyquil to help me go to sleep and get through the night—anything I can do to make the issue go away. I don't recommend it, but it's what I do.

This is what we do with our lives when we have been hurt and our love is infected. We try anything to get by instead of getting to the real issue and securing the proper care. Remember I was just telling you how my father's infection caused the wrong words to come out? He was troubled and perplexed by that. Well, this can happen in relationships, too.

When you would rather say that you love your mate, but something else comes out, this indicates there is an infection somewhere. You go to them intending to apologize, but instead you become defensive.

It's not you; it's the infection talking. When your love has become infected, things change unintentionally. Have you ever been so hurt that, when you wanted to say something sweet to your significant other, you ended up telling them, *you make me sick,* or *you get on my nerves?* You see them and you really want to embrace them, but instead, you go sit on the other side of the room, or on the opposite end of the couch.

When you looked into their eyes in the past, you would get weak from the overwhelming love you felt, but now, you peer at them as if they disgust you. What about their touch? When they used to caress you, it would cause you to melt into their arms, but now you act as if you don't want them to put their hands on you at all. Have you asked yourself *what makes me respond this way?*

Have you ever blurted something out and you knew that wasn't how you honestly felt? Every time you wanted to respond differently—with love in its purest form— you said the opposite of what you were actually feeling. It's bad when you know you don't mean that terrible thing you just said, but you can't seem to stop it from flying out of your mouth. It's like you lose control of your words and actions.

What about those couples that normally do everything together but all of a sudden they don't want to stand next to each other in the shower? They would rather slide down the cold wall just to make sure there is no skin-to-skin contact. These type of responses are signs that some type of infection has set in and it's controlling your behaviors and patterns.

Until you get to the root of the problem, your infected love will not allow you to react to your mate as you typically would. It will make you feel like your relationship is in the gutter.

Gutter

It feels like my heart is in the gutter.

Normally when I see you my heart begins to beat faster,

But now it doesn't even flutter.

I plead with my heart to beat again,

But it lays there in misery,

Because it has lost its best friend.

I scream and say if not this one there's always another,

But my bleeding heart is too overwhelmed,

So it would rather stay in the gutter.

If you have any hope of keeping your relationship out of the gutter, stop letting your infection control you. Take the control back. Nip things in the bud. Draw a line in the sand.

Stop passively accepting these disturbing patterns and demand more of yourself. Make a commitment that you will no longer let your infection spread and deteriorate your relationship.

Don't Fool Yourself

Have you ever met someone who is sick with a bad cold or flu, but they are able to continue daily activities as if nothing is wrong? Because they aren't bedridden, they fool themselves into thinking this is no more than a minor case of the sniffles.

Even if you advise them to get some rest before their body

completely shuts down, they refuse.

Their reply is, *Oh, I will be just fine in a few days.*

It's not that serious.

A few days go by and they are getting worse, but they basically say the same thing: *Give me another few days and I will be as good as new.*

A few days later when you see them, they are really bad off. They're laid up in bed, hacking, aching, taking medicine, doing their best to get some rest. They are utterly miserable and in awful condition. By then, the symptoms are walloping them because they didn't take care of that viral infection.

They didn't manage their symptoms in the beginning. They fooled themselves; they felt that the problem would go away on its own. We tend to do this with our hearts and relationships. But don't fool yourself. Don't delude yourself into thinking this will pass without you addressing it. An issue, without the proper care, is only going to get worse. When infection is present, the body needs assistance to fight it. It won't just vanish.

Are You Misdiagnosing Yourself?

During the Prodromal stage, once your symptoms flare up, it gets painful. The pain response is our body's reaction as it attempts to ward off infection. The physical discomfort and uneasiness can be intense. Fighting hurts, which is why most people don't like to do it.

No one likes pain. Anything we can do to avoid it, we try. We do our best to numb it and mask it before figuring out what's causing it. We try to find the right medicine or home remedy to target and get rid of the pain. But no treatment will be effective until we identify the source of the discomfort.

Have you ever been to the doctor for a toothache? Maybe you thought there was a cavity present, but then you were diagnosed with a sinus infection. Have you ever gone to the physician because of chest pains? Maybe you thought you were having a heart attack, only to be diagnosed with gas.

It may or may not have happened to you, but this sort of thing occurs all the time. Finding out what the problem is, is the first step toward getting the proper help. Infected love will make you look at everyone else as if *they* are the problem when it's *you*.

Are you misdiagnosing yourself? Are you looking over your shoulder, to your left, and to your right, when you should be staring in the mirror?

If your love is infected and you don't know the real cause, you will wrongly assess situations. You'll be like someone that isn't good in mathematics doing mental math instead of using a calculator. You'll come up with the wrong answers to the problems.

Miscalculations, misperceptions and misdiagnoses will cause you to misconstrue the intentions of the one you love. For example, when your love is infected, you'll look at the loyal man or woman that actually loves you and view them as someone unfaithful.

Your trust issues are symptomatic of your infection.
Here is a list of wrong diagnoses that come from you playing doctor with your love and relationship:

- We don't spend enough time together so I think something else is going on. But the real problem is that, because you grew up feeling neglected and felt that no one loved you or paid attention to you, you are now needy. So no matter how much time is spent with you, it will not be enough.

- You think you are spending way too much time with the other person and you need space when you are hardly spending any time at all. This could stem from a past relationship where you were controlled in everything you did. Now you have made up your mind that it will never happen again. So you demand your space and end up being distant.

- Let's say you are beautiful and smart, but you struggle with low self-esteem and insecurities. You complain that your partner doesn't compliment you enough. Could it be that you were, in the past, put down and told you would never be much of anything? If so, in your relationship you constantly need validation and praise, but you don't realize the problem lies within.

- What about the young man that grew up in a home where his father, whom he loved dearly, left him at an early age? The result is that he is afraid of commitment.

He hides behind the pain of his past and refuses to commit as not to give anyone else the opportunity to neglect or abandon him like his dad did.

Before you move on to the next chapter:

Think about some of the things you feel are wrong with your partner.

- Now, instead of trying to figure out what they need to do to correct it, honestly assess how *you* could be part of the problem. This exercise takes maturity.
- In your journal, write down the issues *you* have that may be contributing to the rockiness of the relationship.

CHAPTER 9

Be Careful Who You Run To

We know infections can be undetectable, festering just beneath the surface. Given the right environment, they grow and spread to other areas of your life. To keep things under control, go through the process of detection, which is finding and figuring out what's going wrong.

Let's use another medical illustration. Have you ever been to the emergency room where you were told you didn't have a problem and sent home without any medication? Even though you explained your symptoms, there was still no medicine administered. Why?

There was something going on that the General Attending Physician could not see. A specialist, who is trained and has experience with the exact illness causing your symptoms could see and treat it.

A General Physician, however, can't always identify specific ailments the way a highly specialized doctor can. Here's the lesson: when trying to detect an infection before it spreads, we must be careful who we run to for help. Just because someone's intent is good does not mean they are the perfect person to assist you. Their advice or approach may or may not be best-suited to your needs.

See, you have people with all sorts of opinions. Some will say *hold on* and others will say *let go*. Who should you listen to? With varying thoughts and ideas from the wrong sources swirling around in your head, it becomes even more challenging to make the right call.

Sometimes you'll hear someone tell you, *you'll be okay* or *don't worry about it; it will get better*. But that's not enough. You need a well-informed second opinion from someone equipped to help you get to the root of the problem. Otherwise, you will be left in a worse state. Be sure whoever is leading you is qualified to do that. Above all else, seek God for guidance. He will show you the way.

Discover Your Mate's Love Language

By this point, you are no longer able to hide emotions. If there is trouble in the camp, you and your significant other already realize, "Houston, we have a problem." Now it's time to be about the business of resolving the problem.

So, how can you do it? Gary Chapman, author of the book

entitled *Understanding the Five Love Languages,* is one of those qualified sources to go to for help.

He has created an excellent tool to steer you in the right direction. According to him, the five love languages are:

1. Words of affirmation
2. Acts of service
3. Receiving gifts
4. Quality time
5. Physical touch

I recommend borrowing from his method if you and your partner are experiencing strife and feeling let down in the relationship. Your negative emotions may be a key indicator that you do not understand each other's love language. This simply means you don't have a firm grasp on what the other's needs are or how they most prefer to have love expressed.

How many times do you tell your mate how well they have

done something each day? Do you show your appreciation and let them know how valuable they really are? Just saying thank you goes a very long way, you know.

Being affirming is one of the necessary steps in helping save and improve your relationship. If you are interested in getting better in this area, go for it. But don't stop there. Make sure you know what your partner wants. To find out, communication is necessary, because understanding love languages is a two-way street. It requires two-person participation. It must be communicated and reciprocated by both parties in order to be effective.

Before you move on to the next chapter:

If both you and your partner are willing to do the work, ask yourself: *do we have someone trustworthy we both feel comfortable going to?*

- If you've needed help for a while, what has stopped you from seeking it out?

- Get ready to talk to your partner about taking the next steps and getting wise advice from a qualified source.

CHAPTER 10
Don't Play the Comparison Game

Another manifestation of infection is the incessant need to compare your relationship to other couples' relationships. How often do you look at other relationships and say to yourself *I want that for my relationship?*

Being inspired by the strength of someone else's union is never a bad thing. But it could become unhealthy if you are comparing your partner's attributes to someone else's and drawing the conclusion that, *I want a woman or a man like that*. No two relationships are ever just alike, so coveting what someone else has is dangerous.

That unhealthy longing for what isn't yours makes you overlook the special, unique things about *your* mate and relationship. It puts someone else and their bond on a pedestal. It minimizes the important things you and your partner share. Don't play the comparison game.

Respecting another couple that you can learn from or commending their longevity is great. Just don't look at their union in a covetous way. It does not benefit you to idolize those who appear to have everything together and start wanting to recreate what you see in them. Each connection is distinct. Besides, you have no clue about what it took for that other couple to get where they are.

Comparing your mate to someone else's is a sure way to start an infection in your heart, as well as in the mind of your partner. If you have been heading down this road, make a U-Turn. Stop basing your relationship on other relationships. Catch this comparison infection early and stop it in its tracks.

What works for them may not work for you. Just like fingerprints, their relationship cannot be duplicated. Focus on what you have. Rely on God. Be thankful for the mate He blessed you with. Find the praiseworthy attributes of the one you love and build from there.

If you work hard on your relationship, you won't have time to gaze at someone else's. You'll be too busy improving your love life to notice what everybody else is doing. Often, we are influenced by what we saw our parents or guardians do while growing up. This is how most of us learned about life.

Whether the example they set was good or bad, you still

have to find your own way. I am not discrediting good examples, but I am saying that we can't run our relationship the way anyone else runs theirs. Learn to march to your own beat by doing what works well for you. If you imitate others, you will never discover the full potential of your own relationship. You will never enjoy the sweet, unique fruit that grows from your own seeds planted in your private garden. God has made each of us different because He intended for us to operate in our own special way.

Letting so many other examples rule your life and your relationship will continually cause division and hardship. If you want to enjoy life, get to know yourself and your mate. Embrace your uniqueness.

The Invasive Phase

You are now at the third stage of infection known as the Invasive or Acute Phase. This is when bacteria rapidly multiplies and reaches its highest rate of growth.

Symptoms are most severe at this point because the immune system is fighting the hardest. By now, the infection has taken over surrounding tissues and the agent has been identified. In many cases, if someone gets to this stage, that means they went for a long time without knowing what was going on in their body. By the time they discovered it, they were already in bad shape.

In relationships, often, too much time passes without us understanding what has been happening in our hearts. Therefore, the infection has had time to do major damage. That's why I stress the importance of focusing on your relationship and not playing the comparison game. Looking at someone else's life distracts you. It keeps you from paying attention to the health of your own relationship.

When you are distracted, infection takes over and does severe damage. This can affect your spouse, children, job and primarily you. Gazing longingly at what someone else has won't fix your problems. Your distractedness actually helps the infection become more aggressive and affect everything around you.

Before you know it, "It's complicated" becomes more than a Facebook status telling your social media followers your relationship is in trouble. Those two words end up perfectly summarizing the treatment process once your infection has spread.

When the invasive toxins are no longer localized or confined to one area, treatment becomes significantly more challenging. Things get complicated. In the acute phase of infection, infected love easily takes over our relationships and sucks out the life and vitality. Something must be done—fast—before it's too late.

Are you noticing acute symptoms in your relationship? Have your issues started spreading from just one thing to multiple things? Are you fighting over money, intimacy, children, and other household decisions? If you see symptoms that make you think you may be in the invasive period, it's going to take extra work, prayer, patience and diligence to save the union.

Watch Out for those Mind Games

Infection begins in the mind. Oftentimes, past hurtful experiences live on for years in our brain. We remember what the trauma felt like and the lingering pain it caused.

Those haunting incidents mentally reawaken us to the devastation and heartbreak. The imprint on our psyche, which is already difficult to erase, deepens. Our thoughts become cluttered. Our opinions and perceptions are controlled by our negative history. We look at our mate through jaundiced eyes. We don't trust. We compare.

The mind games start. The memories toy with us. Suddenly, our present is controlled by our past. We let our history negatively impact our destiny. We live in the land of "what if" and "they might." Once that infection has spread and taken over, it's easy to make up unfounded scenarios.

Have you ever had an internal war based entirely on what if scenarios? *What if she was trying to talk to my man?* All of a sudden, you see yourself snatching off your earrings, taking off your shoes and pulling your hair back into a bun. You go through this whole simulation in your mind and this young lady doesn't even know who your man is!

This is when you know that your mind has really been infected. When you are in a crowded room and find yourself trying to guess who your significant other has been talking to, this will drive you crazy.

This infection of mistrust will spread from your mind to your emotions and take you for a roller coaster ride that won't end. Your moods and the relationship will have lots of ups and downs. Things will remain unhealthy and unstable.

Get to the Bottom of Things

Why needs to become your new favorite question. Probing into your history is beneficial. And at this phase it is honestly crucial. You need to get to the bottom of things before the infection becomes uncontainable and incurable.

Ask yourself: why do I feel this way? Why am I comparing my relationship to others' so often? Why do I tell myself over and over again not to act or respond in this manner, but I still do it? Why do I coach myself and convince myself that I will not react negatively to made-up scenarios, no matter how I feel, only to lose self-control in the end?

When you have been infected emotionally and mentally, it is almost impossible to produce any other reaction than the one caused by your illness. Your response is symptomatic of your disease.

Have you noticed that when you have the stomach flu the

symptoms are uncontrollable? You don't make the decision to regurgitate, have headaches, a fever, body aches, and loss of appetite. The infectious virus forces these reactions, even if you don't want to have them. No matter how hard you try to cover it up, someone is guaranteed to notice something's not right with you and ask, *what's wrong? Why are you in this condition?*

Infection, at this stage, has taken over. Your emotions are in the driver's seat now. All control is lost. Your heart and mind have been completely infected by the toxicity that has spread to vital parts of your heart and consciousness.

It's tough when the infection advances and consumes the heart, too. Suddenly, your ability to think clearly is gone. You make rash, irrational decisions. Your mate no longer matters because of the infection that is present.

You see the hurt in your children's eyes because of how you act and what you say, but that is not your concern. Your heart has turned to stone from the effects of the sickness. The blood doesn't pump adequately anymore to maintain life. Many people give up here, because the fight feels unbearable.

Don't Quit Now

The invasive, acute stage is brutal, but the relationship does not have to end. Don't quit now. This all could be fixed and made whole again with some hard work. You can still live, save your relationship and family at this point. But your infected mind causes you to think only defeated thoughts.

It's not that you don't love your partner anymore. You just have allowed yourself to become a prisoner in your mind and this is contributing to your relationship's demise. This is the exact stage where infidelity, abuse and neglect happens. All the worst thoughts and actions you allowed to sit in the incubator of your mind have spread.

Nevertheless, despite how bad it's gotten, healing is yet possible. But just as an infection needs antibiotics, you need treatment.

Before you move on to the next chapter:

It's time to do more self-evaluating.

- Ask yourself, *do I want to be whole? Am I resistant to change or am I willing to go through the process of fighting this infection in my relationship?*

- Be honest. If you want to be whole, you must have true resolve and commitment to get through the grueling process.

CHAPTER 11
Follow Through

Don't try to cover it. Treat it. You can't cure this with a band aid. If you try, the infection is going to get worse and cause the wound to become larger. As your flesh deteriorates, it will begin to smell bad and your cover-up will be exposed.

If you know your love has been infected but you're trying to heal it with a smile, as you're putting up a front, the hurt is growing deeper. The pain and emotional stench will be alarming to those you come into contact with. Remember, as I said earlier, once the infection has been identified, get the right help.

So what's the proper course of action to cure the infection? Glad you asked. Treat it aggressively. Take antibiotics in order to kill the infection. And the key here is to follow directions.

Let's say you have some sort of viral infection that can only be treated with a prescribed antibiotic. The doctor tells you to take the medicine every day for the next 7 to 10 days. He says you must adhere to the instructions and don't stop your treatment until the medicine is completely gone. You might nod your head in compliance and start out with good intentions.

But if you are like me, you don't always perfectly obey doctor's orders. I have had antibiotics and gotten sidetracked. In the past, I've even forgotten to take the medicine or missed the right time to self-administer my dosage.

For the sake of our example, let's pretend you're a bad

patient, even a little worse than me. Maybe you skip dosages often or stop treatment prematurely after you're feeling a bit better, despite knowing you're supposed to finish off the bottle. This is an error! The infection could return because you didn't follow doctor's orders. Follow-through is important.

For very specific treatments, you have to get on a schedule without veering from the regimen. You are ordered to take the antibiotic at the same time each day. If you happen to skip a dosage, the directions are to resume dosages the next day to be back on schedule.

Be Consistent

Apathy and laziness will allow the toxic relationship-killers to thrive. So follow all the way through with the directions and be consistent. Don't do the right thing for a day or two, quit, and then expect for everything to be amazing. Obey doctor's orders and be consistent with your love, loyalty, faithfulness, care, honesty, protection, provision, intimacy, happiness, support, affection, time, communication, excitement, patience, and understanding. Most of all, nourish your relationship with God. He will give you the strength, clarity and wisdom you need to prevent infection from taking over.

Right here, take a moment to think about your situation. Consider where you are and assess how your relationship is going. If you have stopped doing what it takes to bring healing to your relationship and to your heart, why?

Do you really want to see restoration take place and experience a real improvement in your relationship? Things can get better, though it might be hard to believe that today. I do understand that sometimes it *seems* impossible for your issues to be rectified. And this might be true in extreme cases. But there are many instances when problems seem irreconcilable when they really are not. It just takes time. Change doesn't happen immediately, but the medicine will work if you give it a chance.

Just as it took time for infected love to spread, it takes time for it to be healed. Things can turn a corner if you stay on the journey and be consistent, even when you're frustrated and don't know what to do.

Think about what you can do differently every day, starting today, to improve your relationship. Stick to it and don't go back on your commitment. It won't get better suddenly, but if you work at it, your effort will pay off.

Your Make-or-Break Point

I thought we had made it,

But I was only being played with.

I'm tired of being mad, really I hate this.

Always smiling, I'm tired of faking it.

You say that you love me, but how can you say this?

My heart is broken and I can't shake it.

Back and forth, ups and down, I can't take it.

If you think I am here for games, you're mistaken.

If this is a game to you, you're the only one playing.

I know marriage is honorable because God's Word says it.

Unfortunately, it seems like I'm the only one who read this.

I am trying to break free but the mud is too thick,

I have a lot of answers, but not for this.

The words you just read are the sentiments of someone at the make-or-break stage. Are you there right now? If so, you know where the hurt, pain, depression and guilt comes from. The question at hand is, *what are you going to do about it?*

As you've learned already, infection doesn't go away on its own. It takes proper treatment. Depending on how severe the infection is, you may need to undergo an aggressive process. If you see infection trying to take over, and your relationship is in critical condition, there is hope. Yes, it is still worth fighting for. It's time for a focused, no-nonsense, relentless treatment plan. That's what you need.

What would that plan entail, you ask? How would you go about remedying the problem? How could there possibly be a solution tailor-made for this phase? The advanced treatment you need would consist of counseling, communicating, putting your emotions aside and opening up your heart to acknowledge the good, the bad, and the ugly—together.

Be aware that if you don't put in the work, infidelity, anger, drug and alcohol abuse, verbal wars, isolation and depression can start. Sadly, splitting up may be the ultimate result. To avoid this, it is imperative that you get help to get your emotions in check and salvage your struggling relationship.

The Convalescent Stage

Most of us have heard of a convalescent home where people go for rehabilitation after a stroke or another debilitating injury. They end up there because they survived something physically traumatic and need help getting back to 100 percent.

If you do the hard work of fighting infection, you can reach the fourth and final stage, which is known as the *Convalescent Stage*. This is the phase of recovery where you are gradually, over time, becoming healthy and strong again. You're getting better one day at a time.

When you have the flu and you take the proper medication, and get plenty of rest, the symptoms start to go away. Eventually, you begin feeling better. The fever lets up. Your appetite returns. There are no more headaches and muscle aches. Although you feel weak and the body does not feel fully recovered, if you continue to follow the doctor's instructions, you will return to full strength soon.

Relationships tend to work the same way. We all would like for the pain to instantly leave. The truth is, no one likes hurting. We would love for the infection to vanish without having to take medicine. No one clicks their heels together and celebrates the flu or a bad cold. The bottom line is this: sickness doesn't feel good to anyone—in your body or in your relationship.

Nobody revels in having emotional struggles, being broken-hearted and experiencing relationship turmoil. We all want quick remedies to get rid of discomfort. But expedited recovery isn't always a possibility.

Depending on how bad the infection is, it may take longer to heal and that's okay. The positive side of all of this is, with time and the proper care, by degrees, you'll be healthy again. You can make a full recovery.

Before you move on to the next chapter: Ask yourself, *what would recovery look like to me in my relationship?* Write the answer down in your journal and be as specific as possible.

CHAPTER 12

Know When It's Over

Notice in the previous chapter that I said *you* can make a full recovery. But the reality is, every relationship will not—and does not need to—recover. If the other person is carrying an infection and doesn't want to be whole, there is no way to improve things. It takes two.

So, in such a case, it would be better to get rid of the cause of the infection instead of hanging on. Staying connected to someone who is infected and is pleased to remain that way, will only infect you.

Know when it's over. If you have to split up, you will still need to fight the infection you caught from your unhealthy partner. There are a few things that need to happen to start your full recovery.

Target the Infection

Tackle your issues head-on. Your infection may be hurt, rejection, abuse, neglect, distrust, low self-esteem or depression. The first step for you would be making a firm commitment to do everything you can to target and prevent the infection from overtaking your life. Be resolved that you will get better.

Push Yourself

Most times, if you have been hit hard by infection, it will require that you push yourself to eat, drink, move around and get back into your daily routine.

Your body has gone through a severe trauma and it is tired from fighting off the infection. Just take it step-by-step each day. Keep pushing through the tough times and you will fully get back into the swing of things.

Choose a Different Direction

There are many self-help books that give good information. But none of the principles work unless you decide for yourself that you are no longer going to allow this infection to dominate your life. Choose a different direction. Get on a new path. Make a much-needed positive change. You have the power within!

Be Positive

Get excited about your journey. Think new, uplifting thoughts that are not weighed down by what hurt you before. Going backwards is not an option. So be optimistic. Build yourself up. Don't be negative. Quote scriptures. Listen to motivational talks. Believe that a better life is possible.

Leave the Past Behind

Stop rehearsing and replaying all the hurtful events over and over. You have to face the reality that something unfortunate did happen, even if you have not drawn a conclusion as to why. If you don't have the answers, it's okay.

Don't destroy your life over something you may never find out. You have to move on knowing that your life is going to improve from this day onward.

Speak Life

The residue of the type of infection that has gripped your heart and mind can be difficult to erase. But you can do it. Believe that. You must continue to speak life and not death. Tell yourself every day that *God has a good plan for me*. Don't talk about your negative history. Discuss your positive destiny. Your words have power.

Forgive

Forgive whoever you need to forgive, no matter what they did. Don't just concentrate on forgiving the person who hurt you, but also forgive yourself. It's necessary to release any shame, hostility and bitterness so the healing process can truly begin.

Whatever has happened in the recent or distant past, you can get over it and start fresh. I understand things can be so challenging that it seems like you are about to lose your mind, but this is not the case! You have suffered and survived the worst; now it is time to change course. In order for things to be better, you must recommit to doing better.

Occupy your time with new things. Change your surroundings. Attend different events. Be open to fresh ideas and discoveries. Tread paths you may have never walked down before. This is all part of getting your strength back and learning to live again during this time of recovery.

If you have to break off a relationship, I have two words for you: let go. In the beginning it won't be easy. You'll have good days and difficult ones. But releasing that person and ridding your life of toxicity is essential to your growth and happiness.

Give Yourself Permission to Move Forward

Whether you are about to walk away from a relationship that has died from untreated infection, or you are starting fresh in the recovery phase, give yourself permission to move forward. Don't be held hostage by the past. Recover and take a new route. Don't repeat old cycles. Forge your own path. Starting fresh is a beautiful thing.

When the time comes for new love, take time to find out what makes *both* of your hearts sing. See what fills your union with joy and delight. Come together. Create an environment that pleases the two of you. Your methods can't be guided by what someone else—no matter how well-meaning—has dictated to you.

Come up with standards that will uphold your values. Prioritize what's important to you. When you're in a new relationship, or you are rekindling an old flame that burned out, it is awesome to discover each other. At this point, you should be asking each other questions like:

- What upsets you in our relationship?
- How can I change things to make it better?
- How can we work on this together to make us both happy?
- What makes you smile?

- What are some of the things that you like to hear?

- What do I do that you love?

- How can I please you even more?

Uplift your Mate

I remember I was having a bad day. I was cranky and upset because I was trying to take care of some things that I really didn't have the money for.

When my wife saw the frustration on my face, she looked at me and said, "You are an excellent provider." Instantly, the frown I had been wearing turned into a smile. My heart was lifted.

Uplift your mate. Be in tune with their emotions. Try something new. Say something different. This can kindle a new spark. Isn't that what you want? It doesn't make sense to continue doing the same ineffective things, hoping for a new result.

Most times, when we recover from an infection, we take

extra precautions with our health. We become more conscious of those coughing around us. We wash our hands more frequently and keep a bottle of hand sanitizer everywhere we go. These are measures we take to stay infection-free.

The same thing should happen with your love in order to keep *it* healthy. You must be aware of people and things that negatively affected and infected your love in the past. Stay away from those that meant to do you harm. From here forward, it has to be all about uplifting your mate, strengthening your relationship and defining what pure bliss is for you and your significant other.

Watch Out for Red Flags

If you are not currently in a relationship, during the recovery phase, the door may open through which someone new enters. Just make sure you choose wisely before giving your heart to anyone. Pay close attention to any red flags you see before connecting romantically with someone else. Stay emotionally sound so you don't fall victim to your feelings.

If you are presently in a committed relationship that is worth holding on to, then make it work. Embrace the joy of newness. Protect your happiness. You should watch out for any red flags, too. Old habits die hard.

Don't fall back into those cycles, routines and patterns that proved detrimental to the health of your love before. When it comes to what you say and how you behave, be mindful.

Communicate with one another about any challenges that arise. An open line of communication is the best way to maintain a healthy relationship and hold on to that blissfulness. You'll be amazed by how wonderful things can be.

Things

Things don't look the same anymore

Things don't appear the same as they did before.

Things don't grip my heart to the core

Things that used to rule me can't anymore.

Things no longer have my heart sore

Things from past hurts have now become a bore.

Things that seemed as if they were on auto-save and stored

Are things that I have now deleted that I don't have use for.

Things have brought me new life

Things have shown me a new light.

Things have displayed to me a greater opportunity

Things have shown the true beauty in me.

You have the Power

In recovery, it becomes clear that you have the power to be happier and more in love than you were before. If you tap into that power, you will enjoy longevity and contentment in your relationship.

Any toxic behaviors and attitudes must be blocked and stopped immediately from spreading. Love from a pure place. You most certainly have it in you. All of us desire to experience happiness in our relationship, but all of us do not tap into our power to create that happiness and joy. But why not? We were created to love because God is love. He wants us to have joy in our relationship. We already have what we need to build a lasting, loving, nurturing union. We just have to do it.

The best type of love is a love that is not infected. It is a love that flows through a heart that is fully recovered, tender and open. If you have gotten this far reading *Infected Love*, that means you have a desire to experience happiness and healthiness in your love life. You have the grit, willpower and determination to do the serious work it takes to have the kind of relationship you want. Use your power. As the popular expression goes, "Ain't nothing to it but to do it."

Patience is a Virtue

In this phase, things may be looking up, but that doesn't mean the work has ended. You still will need to do what is necessary to fully recover and heal from past hurts, so you can continuously experience the true beauty of love.

Be patient. Everything won't be perfect every day. Building a new and stable foundation takes time. As the saying goes, "Rome wasn't built in a day" and a strong relationship with yourself and your mate can't be built in a day either. I know we all like fast results. We want immediate satisfaction. But patience is a virtue that many of us don't have.

Take me for instance. I like to eat as soon as I am hungry. Instead of waiting for a home-cooked meal, I prefer to stop by a fast food restaurant and simply grab my food to go. I like to have it within five minutes instead of two hours. What I obtain quickly, however, isn't always the best quality. It simply satisfies the craving for instant gratification.

Because of my impatient impulse eating, at one point, my health began to deteriorate. I developed high blood pressure and became overweight. Going for the quick fix stopped me from consuming the kinds of foods I needed to keep me healthy.
After my health took a turn for the worst, it forced me to do something different. I reassessed my habits based on what doctors said. I began preparing my own meals. I started making everything from scratch.

These days, even when I want to indulge in some sweet treats, I no longer buy boxed cake mix or frosting. Everything is made from scratch. It tastes so much better and I know exactly what is going into my body. Does it take more time? Yes. But is it worth it? Absolutely!

I knew my love affair with fast food had to end if I wanted

to be healthy. If you have been in a toxic relationship, you know something has to change if you want to change your life for the better as well.

If a relationship is infected, know when it's over and don't be afraid to start fresh. And when you do embark on a new journey with a new person, apply all the wisdom you learned in that previous failed relationship to make your new love the best love ever.

Before you move on to the next chapter: Learning new ways of doing things isn't always simple. Keep your expectations grounded in reality.

Both you and your mate are only human and mistakes will be made. But, there are boundaries in your recovery phase that must never be crossed.

- Right now, list out a few patterns, behaviors and cycles you need to be extra mindful of, so you don't repeat them.

CHAPTER 13
Teamwork Makes the Dream Work

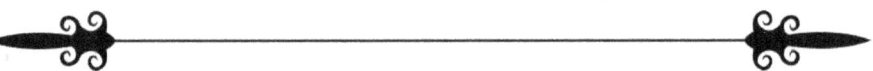

As I mentioned in the previous chapter, in our relationships we want everything to happen fast, but it won't. You cannot choose a TV-dinner-mate, expecting the results of a home-cooked-meal-man or woman. It's going to take a little more time to get the results you're looking for. Give that person ample time to grow, develop and change for the better.

Don't get aggravated when things don't happen quickly and

don't get frustrated when issues don't resolve overnight. Be unified. You are partners in love. Togetherness is essential to growth and success in your relationship. Teamwork makes the dream work. Whether you face communication challenges or money problems, unity and patience are the keys to a relationship's longevity and health. If your partner was financially strapped before you got them, why are you expecting them to take care of all of the bills in the beginning of the marriage?

Being short on cash or failing to budget properly is an issue that plagues many couples in numerous households. Instead of getting angry, be supportive. Both of you must work together to get more income into the house.

Do a better job of budgeting and come up with a financial plan. Again, teamwork makes the dream work. Tackle the issue together. Double-team the problem instead of fighting each other. Calculate expenses and be realistic about your goals.

Instead of arguing, encourage one another. Put your heads together and discover strategic ways to meet your objectives. See how that works? You and your mate are partners in everything. If you have a willingness to wait, make incremental changes and work together, everything will be alright.

They Won't Always Get it Right

When it comes to having your needs met in the relationship, your mate won't do everything right every day. Perhaps your partner isn't giving you the attention you need. Don't argue. Don't give them the cold shoulder. Take time to communicate and sometimes, simply lead by example, without being overly assertive and overbearing.

Keep in mind that it will take a while to adapt to new methods. It's not impossible to experience what you wish to see. But often, it requires more time than we are willing to give. Be patient, understanding, and expect them to make some mistakes. Be in it for the long haul. Don't try to rush things if you want to stay together. If you are committed to spending the rest of your lives with one another, know that learning to build and grow is a process.

A store-bought pound cake does not compare to a homemade pound cake. The rich taste of the one made from scratch is undeniably superior. It also takes more time to bake it than buy it. If you want your relationship to be rich and enjoyable, let it bake a while. Stop pushing for everything to be perfect right away. Go the distance.

P.A.U.S.E.

As you're working on being more patient and building the relationship as a team, there are things you can do to make the process easier. Take time out and P.A.U.S.E. This is an acronym I have created:

P -*Pray* and ask God for more patience, clarity and direction. If you petition Him for wisdom and understanding, He will give it to you.

A -*Accept* that the journey will take time and this process will have both ups and downs. Embrace it. You're headed somewhere beautiful.

U-*Unify* with your mate. Stick closely by their side. Let togetherness be your goal. Let them know you are with them and willing to work and patiently trust that things will get better over time.

S-*Share* your feelings, hopes and dreams for your relationship with your partner. Even as you endure the rough places, keep your goals out front. This will give you something to work toward together.

E-*Encourage* each other along the way. Celebrate successes and milestones—both great and small. You both are in this until death do you part.

Slow Down and Spend Some Alone Time

Even though working together is important, there are some things you must do alone. It's necessary to slow down and check in with yourself. During me-time, you can cultivate habits to help you along the journey of making sure your love is not infected.

At least twice a week or more, spend time getting to know yourself. Often, we are so consumed with catering to someone else, that we forget about ourselves. Slow your pace. Give yourself some time and attention.

Self-care and carving out room for you is an important part of remaining happy and whole. Work on personal growth and development, recognizing that you, too, need to mature in the relationship.

Instead of wasting energy being upset with your mate because you feel like they don't know you, how about getting to know yourself first? Don't focus on relationship issues and neglect personal issues. Being alone is great for you, as it can reveal unhealthiness in you first, and your relationship second.

Slowing down and enjoying alone time allows you to think. You'll begin to see things clearly and differently. Sometimes, simply have a cup of coffee or tea, or maybe your favorite dessert, accompanied by a good book. Whatever it takes to release your mind and let go of preoccupation, do it.

Find out what makes you happy and joyful. For you, it could be going to a movie or shopping. Maybe it's just a change of scenery you need. How about getting outside of those four walls and taking a walk around the neighborhood, or through a local park?

Relax. This is when you can breathe, reassess and reexamine things. As the saying goes, hindsight is 20/20. No one ever said how far a thing has to be behind you in order to see it clearly. Sometimes all it takes is a little time to clear your mind.

Pray Without Ceasing

Even though the two of you are working together, there are some things only prayer can do. Prayer should never be a last resort; it must always be your first line of defense against infection.

1 Thessalonians 5:17 says, "Pray without ceasing." Every day, all day, it takes prayer to keep you. Of all the actions you take, communicating with God is the most important one. As you work on your relationship and wait to see positive changes, there are specific prayers you should pray.

Her Prayer

Dear Heavenly Father, thank You for another opportunity to get it right. I don't have all the answers to questions concerning how to fix my relationship, but You do. I surrender myself to You.

Give me wisdom on how to love. As it says in Your word, Proverbs 31:10-11, "An excellent wife who can find? She is more precious than jewels. The heart of her husband trusts in her, and he will have no lack in gain."

Lord, help me to uphold Your word in my heart, that I will be the woman that You intended for me to be. In Jesus' name, Amen.

His Prayer

Dear Heavenly Father, thank You for another opportunity to get it right. I don't have all of the answers to fix my relationship, but You do. I surrender myself and my relationship to You.

Give me wisdom on how to love. As it says in your word in Ephesians 5:25, "Husbands, love your wives, as Christ is the head of the church and gave himself up for her." Let me love sacrificially and not superficially, so that I will honor both You and my wife in all I say and do daily.

In Jesus' name, Amen.

After you have prayed and released your issues to the Lord, you will have a new testimony of freedom.

Freedom

Wow, I can breathe now.

Just a little while ago I couldn't see how.

Yes, I can see again,

My life was so dark, I wanted it to end.

Thank God the sun is shining,

All my troubles are now behind me.

Now I can focus on my future,

My bleeding heart has now been sutured.

I never thought this day would come,

Oh but I thank God, thank God for my freedom!

No More Toxicity

You have been equipped to fight infection and win. So walk away from this reading experience with a new determination. Commit to toxic-free living.

Whatever you need to say and do, and whatever steps you need to take toward success in your relationship, do it. Be uninhibited. Walk in your freedom. Tap into the pure joy and bliss that can now be found inside your pure, infection-free heart. No more toxicity is your new motto.

You have taken in all the information you need to be free of infection. Don't just close the book and forget what you have read. Reference *Infected Love* continually to fortify and protect your heart, and your relationship.

It is a defense tool to keep toxic things that threaten to kill your love out of your life. Hold on to the principles. Store them in your heart and mind, and you will see firsthand what it's like to enjoy a healthy, infection-free relationship.

It's possible for you!

Acknowledgements

Thank you to all of my wonderful children: Dominique, Donisha, Erin, Katlyn, Dion Jr., Davin, Myles, and Olivia who have given me the will to write this book. I hope it helps you in your relationships.

To my parents, Bishop Joseph Sr. and Annie Brinson who demonstrated what a sound relationship looks like when you are not only in love, but committed.

To my brother, Joseph Brinson III, who designed my book cover and lent his wonderful artistic insight to the creative process.

To my sister, Dianna Hobbs, and her company, Hobbs Ministries Publishing, for publishing my book. I couldn't have done it without you.

To my sister Laquinte' Brinson, who I bothered often for feedback and suggestions, thank you for your consistent help.

To all my siblings and friends who took time to read my book and give encouraging words to admonish me to continue to write.

And finally, to everyone who contributed in any way, I appreciate you.

About the Author

Dion Brinson Sr. is a devoted husband to Kimberly and a proud father of 8 children. His passion to see people thrive both personally and in their relationships has led him to devote his life to the empowerment of others.

The Christian entrepreneur, author and public speaker holds a Bachelor's degree in Biblical Studies from O.L. Meadows School of Ministry and resides in Alabama with his family.

www.ingramcontent.com/pod-product-compliance
Lightning Source LLC
Chambersburg PA
CBHW060134100426
42744CB00007B/781

Chapter 1 The Best Student Debt Solution

Congress must have the will to act

There are many solutions for student loan debt at different levels discussed in this book. The first and the best solution is depicted in the title of the book: *Wipe Out All Student Loan Debt Now!* It is clearly the ideal solution from an American point of view and it has economic ramifications that along with the new tax plan can add to a major jump re-starting of the economy. The ideal solution would be to wipe out all of the student debt from all college loans. There are many ways the US can afford this and prosper because of it.

This act alone would free forty-five million debt-ridden former college students, mostly graduates to go ahead and get real lives for themselves. They will be in a position to start a business, buy a home, a new car, and begin a family.

The negative impact of so many student borrowers is clear. Essentially, the US has 45 million Americans, who are putting a big chunk of their monthly income towards their student debts. That means that they aren't spending on other economy-boosting goods or services. This group also has less money to save, invest, or even start a business. The burden is so heavy that over 8 million (and growing) have stopped paying a dime. This phenomenon is called being in default.

Three other Opinions on canceling Student Loan Debt

I am not the only person who thinks it is a good idea to start over again on student loans and wipe what we have off the books as soon as possible. Here are three other opinions as to why it is not only a good idea; it is a great idea and the US can not only afford it; the country will profit from it.

David Muccigrosso, an Armchair Economist, blogging at //www.quora.com, on Feb 12, 2013 took a shot at answering this important question: *What would be the economic impact of forgiving all US student loan debt?*

At the time this was written in 2013, student loans and debt in the US exceeded credit card debt, at just over $1 trillion. Now the debt is closer to $1.45 trillion because there have been no major changes made by colleges and universities to assure new student debtors will be able to pay back their loans. Here is David's piece:

> "Around 80% of that is guaranteed by the federal government, with the rest belonging to private lenders.
>
> "Theoretically, winding down all student loan debt would proceed like a national, publicly organized bankruptcy. The federal government would start by forcing lenders to take a "haircut" (significant discount to outstanding principle) on the loans it's guaranteed, and it would allow private loans to be consolidated as federal loans for the purpose of being put through this program as well.
>
> "Winding down $1 trillion in debt is hard in any circumstance. This will be even harder given the sheer amount of bitching the financial sector already does about the federal government. The program would probably take from $500 to $800 billion in total spending (equating to a 50-20% haircut for investors) - roughly the same magnitude as the Bush stimulus package.
>
> "Most banks would not be crippled, but the financial sector would still have a hard time dealing with the hit to their balance sheets...
>
> "The other major problem would be that a program of this magnitude would destroy the student lending market as we know it. Higher education finance would have to be replaced by a spending package on the order of at least $1 trillion and involving some higher taxes to provide free universal public higher education - the only real option once you've taken debt-financed education off the table. (TBH, I'm actually in favor of a less dramatic version of this whole wind-down and conversion, but this incarnation is just too unworkable)

"On the plus side, those suffering under student loan burdens would have a lot of income freed up. You'd probably see surges in multifamily unit construction (apt buildings), the auto industry, and nightlife/entertainment spending, but the economic activity wouldn't cancel out the huge Wall Street shit fit that would be simultaneously occurring.

Forgive student loan debt to stimulate the economy.

Originally Written – January 29, 2009
By – Robert Applebaum at http://studentdebtcrisis.org

Back in 2009, President Obama signed into law a $787 billion stimulus package on top of Bush's grossly mismanaged $700 billion TARP bailout from September. That is more than the total student debt of today, $1.45 trillion.

Shortly thereafter in 2009, the Federal Reserve basically printed an additional $1,000,000,000,000 to inject more funds into the monetary system, which will undoubtedly have the effect of diminishing the purchasing power of the dollar. Now, we are approaching twice the total of all the student debt. In other words, if we acted then to forgive the debt, it would be all gone, and all paid for.

Since then, the US government has paid out trillions of dollars in bailouts, handouts, loans and giveaways, with no end in sight as our leaders tried to do anything and everything to get our spiraling economy under control. While some of what Washington has already done may act to stimulate the economy, much of the trillions of dollars already spent will, no doubt, has proven to be just money wasted.

Tax rebate checks do not stimulate the economy – history shows that people either spend such rebates on paying off credit card debt, or they simply save them, doing little to nothing to stimulate the economy. Presumably, that is why they were removed from the final version of the stimulus bill.

The tax cuts that were included, however, amount to a whopping $44 per month for the rest of 2009, decreasing to an even more staggering $33 per month in 2010. This is hardly "relief" as it is likely to help nobody.

The Wall Street financial institutions, auto manufacturers, insurance companies and countless other irresponsible actors received TRILLIONS of taxpayer dollars (as demonstrated above, that's a number with *12* zeros at the end of it) to bail them out of their self-created mess. This, too, did nothing to stimulate the economy. It merely rewarded bad behavior and did nothing to encourage institutional change.

There is a better way.

How many times have we heard from our leaders in Washington that education is the key to solving all of our underlying societal problems? The so-called "Silver Bullet." For decades, presidents, senators and members of Congress have touted themselves as champions of education, yet they've done nothing to actually encourage the pursuit of one on an individual level.

Some of us have taken advantage of Federal Stafford Loans and other programs, including private loans, to finance higher education, presumably with the understanding that an advanced degree equates with higher earning power in the future. Many of us go into public service after attaining such degrees, something that's also repeatedly proclaimed as something society should encourage.

Yet, the debt we've accrued to obtain such degrees have crippled our ability to reap the benefits of our educations, causing many to make the unfortunate choice of leaving public service so as to earn enough money to pay off that debt.

Our economy is still in the tank, though with Trump already we are seeing great signs of relief. There isn't a reasonable economist alive who doesn't believe that the economy has needed a real stimulus for a real long time.

The only debate now centers on how to go about doing it. While the new stimulus plan contains some worthy provisions, very little of it will have a significant and immediate stimulating effect on the economy. The Obama Administration itself in 2009, did not expect to see an upsurge in the economy until mid-to-late 2010.

Instead of funneling billions, if not trillions of additional dollars to banks, financial institutions, insurance companies and other institutions of greed that are responsible for the current economic crisis, why is not a better idea to allow educated, hardworking, middle-class Americans to get something in return? After all, they're our tax dollars too!

Forgiving student loan debt would have an immediate stimulating effect on the economy. With Trump, we are already back to 3.3% GDP growth. Who knows what having 45 million ready to spend, millennials reengaged in the economy will do for the country?

Responsible people who did nothing other than pursue a higher education would have hundreds, if not thousands of extra dollars per month to spend, fueling the economy now.

Those extra dollars being pumped into the economy would have a multiplying effect, unlike many of the provisions of the 2009 era stimulus packages. As a result, tax revenues would go up, the credit markets would unfreeze, and many jobs will be created. Consumer spending accounts for over two thirds of the entire U.S. economy and in 2009, consumer spending has declined at alarming, unprecedented rates. Therefore, it stands to reason that the fastest way to revive our ailing economy is to do something drastic to get consumers to spend.

This proposal would quickly revitalize the housing market, the ailing automobile industry, travel and tourism, durable goods and countless other sectors of the economy because the very people who sustain those sectors will automatically have hundreds or, in some cases, thousands of extra dollars per month to spend.

The driving factor in today's economy is fear. Unless and until the middle class feels comfortable enough that they'll have their jobs, health insurance and extra money to spend not only next month, but the month after that, etc., the economy will not, indeed, cannot grow fast enough to stop the hemorrhaging.

Let me be clear. This is not about a free ride. This is about a new approach to economic stimulus, nothing more. To those who would argue that this proposal would cause the banking system to collapse or make student loans unavailable to future borrowers, please allow me to respond. I am in no way suggesting that the lending institutions who carry such debts on their balance sheets get legislatively shafted by having them wiped from their books.

The banks and other financial institutions have already gotten their money regardless because, in addition to the $700 TARP bailout, even more bailout money came their way. This proposal merely suggests that in return for the Trillions of dollars that has been and will continue to be handed over to the banks, educated, hardworking Americans who are saddled with student loan debt should get some relief as well, rather than sending those institutions another enormous blank check.

Because the banks are being handed trillions of dollars anyway, there would be no danger of making funds unavailable to future borrowers.

To avoid the moral hazard that this plan could potentially create, going forward, the way higher education in this country is financed MUST be reformed. Requiring students to amass enormous debt just to receive an education is an untenable approach, as demonstrated by the ever-growing student loan default rates.

Having a loan-based system rather than one based on grants and scholarships or, ideally, public funding, has, over time, begun to have the unintended consequence of discouraging people from seeking higher education at all. That is no way for America to reclaim the mantle of the land of opportunity.

A well-educated workforce benefits society as a whole, not just the students who receive a higher education. It is often said that an undergraduate degree today is the equivalent of a high school diploma 30 or 40 years ago. Accepting the premise as true that society does, in fact, place the same value on an undergraduate degree today as it did on a HS diploma 30 or 40 years ago, then what is the rationale for cutting off public funding of education after the 12th grade?

It seems to me that there is some dissonance in our values that needs to be reconciled. That, however, cannot come to pass until the millions of us already shackled with student loan debt are freed from the enormous economic burdens we're presently carrying.

Many of the vocal nay-sayers to this proposal seem intent on ignoring the fact that Washington will continue to spend trillions of dollars, likely in the form of handing blank checks over to more and more banks, as a way of getting the economy under control. Normative assessments of how things should be, are fine, but they don't reflect reality.

Accepting the premise that Washington will spend Trillions of dollars in unprecedented ways (a good portion of which will just be trial and error, since we're in uncharted waters), what is the argument against directly helping middle class people who are struggling, rather than focusing solely on the banks and other financial institutions responsible for the crisis to begin with?

Further accepting that there is an aggregate amount of outstanding student loan debt totaling approximately $550 Billion, (that's Billion with a B, not a T), [even more in 2017] one is forced to ask again, what is the objection to helping real people with real hardships when all we're talking about is a relative drop in the bucket as compared with what will be spent to dig us out of this hole?

In a perfect world, I share these biases towards personal responsibility and having people pay back what they owe and making good on the commitments they've made. But we don't live in a perfect world and the global economy, not just the U.S. economy, is in a downward spiral, the likes of which nobody truly knows how to fix.

This proposal will immediately free up money for hardworking, educated Americans, giving them more money in their pockets every month, addressing the very real psychological aspects of the recession as much as the financial ones. Is it the only answer? No, of course not. But could it help millions of hardworking people who struggle every month to get by? Absolutely.

Given the economic climate inherited from the Obama years, as well as the plans to spend trillions of additional dollars that have been in the works, one must wonder what is so objectionable about giving a real helping hand to real people with real struggles.

In 2009, the then new Obama Administration was supposed to be about change. Yet, nothing in the economic stimulus package represented a significant departure from the way Washington has always operated – it's merely a different set of priorities on a higher scale, but it's certainly not materially different from any other economic stimulus package passed during the past few decades.

Washington cannot simply print and borrow money to get us out of this crisis. We the People, however, can get this economy moving NOW. All we need is relief from debt that was accrued under the now-false promise that higher education equates with higher earnings.

Free us of our obligations to repay our out-of-control student loan debt and we, the hardworking, middle-class Americans who drive this economy will spend those extra dollars now.

If you believe that there's a better way of climbing out of this economic crisis, one that empowers us to directly spend money, start businesses, free up credit and create jobs, then please join this group and encourage others to do so as well.

There's strength in numbers – the more people to join this group, the louder our voices and the greater the chances of being heard by President Obama and Congress.

Support real change we can believe in!

More Americans Want to Forgive Trillion-Dollar Student Loan Debt Than Want It Repaid

MoneyTips http://www.ajc.com
4:00 p.m. Friday, July 21, 2017 Business and Money news

More Americans believe that we should forgive all federal student debt than feel that the recipients should pay their loans back. In a shocking survey recently conducted by MoneyTips.com, nearly 42% agreed with the statement, I believe President Trump's Department of Education should forgive all federal student debt to help the economy. Less than 37% disagreed, while the remaining 21% neither agreed nor disagreed.

"It is surprising that the majority of the US population supports this measure," says Brandon Yahn, Founder of studentloansguy.com. "Perhaps this student debt burden has spread more across all generations, and popular sentiment is turning the corner as it relates to student debt."

…

While income wasn't a factor, gender seemed to affect people's feelings on this subject, with more women favoring forgiveness over men. 47% of the women agreed or strongly agreed with the statement, while less than 36% of the men felt the same way.

…

Reasoned millennial money expert Stefanie O'Connell, "Women are now more likely than men to get a college degree, which may explain why they would favor student loan forgiveness at higher rates. They're also likely to experience career interruptions due to childbearing and caretaking, which can impede their lifetime earning potential and, consequently, their ability to pay back their loans.

Finally, many of the lucrative jobs that don't require a college degree tend to be in male-dominated fields - carpentry, electrical, etc. - which might explain why more women favor loan forgiveness."

...

Says Student Loan Hero, expert Miranda Marquit, "Many millennials, who thought they were doing the right thing, took on student loan debt only to graduate to an economy where jobs have been scarce, and wages have been mostly stagnant for decades. Gone are the days when you could work for the summer and pay for the following school year.
As a society, we sold a dream and failed to deliver. You can make payments on your loans for decades and barely make headway."
Adds Marquit,

"As a result, these millennials are unable to help the economy in other ways. Research indicates they are putting off financial milestones that come with economy-building benefits.

"All the consumption that comes with things like buying homes and starting families is being lost because the largest generation yet doesn't have money to spare. Student loan forgiveness would go a long way toward helping millennials feel stable enough to take the next steps in their financial lives, as well as even starting businesses."

Chapter 2 No Problem Is Without a Solution

The government is not your friend

Despite self-serving governmental, political, and academic apologists suggesting that there is no real student debt crisis, just ask a recent millennial graduate when they hope to start a family. You better have a lot of time. We keep hearing about a student debt crisis. Yet, politicians continue to argue that there is no student debt crisis though everybody else knows that there is. Perhaps the definition of a crisis can tell us--*a time of intense difficulty, trouble, or danger.*

The fact is that recent students with major loans are having trouble paying them back. The fact is that they have put off major life plans until their personal crisis improves to manageable.

Is the country in crisis? Whether the country is in crisis or not, taxpayers are now on the hook for about $1.45 trillion outstanding in student debt. That makes student debt substantially larger even than credit card debt. Moreover, it's not looking like it's going to get any better in the future. The graduating class of 2017 owed an average of over $37,000, up from less than $30,000 in 2014.

The real problem is many problems

The people that say there is not a student debt crisis suggest that most people will repay their debts though it may take them 10 to 20 years to do it. The real problem, these people believe is the expanding default rate on student loans. Just a couple years ago, the defaulters were at 7 million. Now 8 million no longer pay a dime back.

Your friendly US Department of Education produced a report recently that noted the two-year cohort default rate on student loans increased from 9.1% for FY 2010 to 10% for FY 2011 In 2017, the default rate has already climbed to 11.2% and the average monthly out of pocket student loan payment for a borrower aged 20 to 30 years is $351. That is a good part of a mortgage payment or a nice payment on a family car.

It cannot be argued that more student debtors are falling behind on their federal student loans. The share of Americans at least 31 days late on loans from the U.S. Department of Education ticked up to 18.8 percent as of June 30, up from 18.6 percent the same time last year.

The total in US student loan debt has climbed to $1.45 trillion and as of right now, about 45 million Americans have some student loan debt.

Most experts say the program is operating in crisis mode.

Who's to blame?

The easiest people to blame for these problems are, of course, the students. After all they are the ones who took out the loans. However, like your dad and my dad would say, "What do they know?" That's actually the problem.

For some reason, which I admit has little merit, we here in the US have decided that the norm for every child born in America is to have a college education. Consequently, I would suspect we have the worst electricians, plumbers, and auto mechanics in the world as we basically shut down the technical aspects once taught in high school.

From what I have observed, the richest guys in many towns today run the plumbing businesses, electrical businesses, and of course body shops and vehicle repair shops. My cousin Frank, who is a great guy by the way, made his millions in New Jersey by being the one body shop in his home town. Now, he makes a few bucks in a different way. He bought about 300 acres in a PA county town that is producing fracking oil in a big way.

Guys like cousin Frank are tickled that many of their future competitors opt to get college degrees. It follows that when they have to pay off the loans for those degrees, they will not have the cash to build a new garage in town to compete against cousin Frank. That may help Frank, but it does not help America.

The supposed plusses of having to have a degree, for years has convinced the vast majority of US high schools to dedicate their efforts to getting their students prepared for a college education. With so many in America possessing four-year degrees today, the sheepskin is often worth little more than the cost of the ink and the parchment.

Think about the gal or guy who sat next to you in a number of high school classes. Were they college material? When everybody, regardless of smarts became college material, colleges figured out how to bolster their income by admitting them on probations that could continue for four years.

So, there are many students who put in their four years without being fully admitted and are then kicked out without a degree when it is obvious that they had taken enough courses to prove that they never should have gone to college. Now, these poor souls cannot find enough money to start a landscaping business, so they get a job flipping hamburgers trying to come up with $350 a month to pay off their four-year student loan. Is that a crisis? It sure is.

Somebody in a university and some coffee-breath faculty student advisor who knows colleges are in it for the money, helped convince Johnny or Janie that they could make it whether they should have a degree or not. Consequently, forty-six percent of those that start college dropout before graduating. As hard as it is to believe, one of the major reasons for this is undoubtedly the fact that many should never have been admitted to any self-respecting college in the first place.

But, we may forget sometimes that colleges are a business also and businesses must survive by having customers who can pay their bills. How wonderful for these institutions with no hearts, that Johnny and Janie equally were able to get a guaranteed student loan so that College A could be assured of receiving their full tuition even if neither had a chance for success.

Another part of the problem is that most seventeen and eighteen-year old's have mush brains and they use valedictorians as models when they are trying to eke out a C in Gym class. Yes, all valedictorians will graduate from college unless they rig the game against themselves. But, most high school students sporting a C average ought to try to find a job as a beautician if they have dexterity, or a barber, or an auto mechanic. If they can get into plumbing or become electrical apprentices, their lives are set.

In Northeastern PA, if the McDonalds and Burger King guys get their $15.00 hourly wage, then the fully degreed sociology majors who are out working in kindness industries, will be able to up their salaries by about $10,000 and they can take over the jobs these non-degreed personnel have. Not only can these college grads flip the burgers better in most cases, they can also handle the cash register.

Additionally, management may find a great brain among them and bring them in to a corporate program. So, why the degree and why the student loan for sociology or psychology if you are not headed for a PhD or an MD.

High school 17 and 18-year-old seniors, though they "know everything," are simply not prepared to choose the right college majors. But, since they have "I know everything," cards printed by their buddies in Print Shop or elsewhere to present to anybody offering counsel, it is tough to talk them out of a career in rocket science.

Sociology is the most altruistic major as the graduate gives to others all her life and she makes little more than the horse groomer at the end of town, who never spent a dime to get a degree. Nonetheless, there are other degrees similar to sociology that millennials are encouraged to pursue. For example, many choose majors that align with their passions such as film and video arts, pre-school education, psychology, anthropology, archaeology, fine arts and music. It's great work if you can get it.

Like sociology, the pursuit of knowledge in these majors might be fun and rewarding but they rarely lead to well-paying careers. For that matter, many of the young people who choose these types of careers won't even be able to find jobs. In fact, as of March 2012, 60% of college graduates were unable to find work in their fields of study.

I have seen statistics that suggest that about 80% of college graduates have no choice but to return to the roost and let mom and dad continue paying their big bills in life. No wonder the Democrats think we need illegal aliens to do the jobs in America that Americans never trained themselves to do well.

Colleges and universities are big culprits in the student loan crisis

It is an understatement to suggest that colleges and universities are at least partially to blame for the student debt problem, especially the for-profit schools. Whether they admit it or not, all colleges and universities other than the finest of the well-endowed, are in a competitive business.

Please permit me to tell you a secret that is not such a secret in the boardrooms of our country's most successful universities. It is as clear as day when you follow the prospects of students who matriculate after much consideration. They contemplate whether they should be greeting card designers or plumbers or college graduates.

While they are in such deep thought, a great number of them are enticed by local counselors with affinities to certain colleges or by various program counsellors in universities that need students to enroll to assure revenue. To get the revenue, the counsellors present loans packages that the prospective students cannot ever afford even with a degree in the art of leisure. That is the first reason why there are so many loan defaults.

Traditional 50 and 100 year old colleges and/or universities that would be classified as non-profit endowment based institutions, are more likely to tell the truth to a high-school flunky, who thinks he should go to college. The flunky wants to go to college often because the girlfriend is going to the same college. Many otherwise bad future marriages would be on the verge of collapse today if the admirer was not already rejected by the institution for lack of cranial substance.

Not all traditional non-profit colleges are so appropriate as to actually deny admittance to a poor scholar. *For-profit* colleges and universities are the worst at grubbing for money from the young chump who wants to be a college graduate because his girlfriend is smart enough to be one.

Under the covers, *For-profits'* admissions departments are run as marketing departments. Marketing to students nobody else wants is their mission. The loan amount and the loan default rates are the highest at these institutions of higher-priced learning. When they default, American taxpayers are again left holding the debt bag, even though the institution is private.

As an example, students that borrow similar amounts to pay for their schooling end up defaulting at a much higher rate at for-profit institutions. In fact, 26% of for-profit students that took out loans between $5000 in $10,000 ended up defaulting versus the 10% of students at community colleges that defaulted and the 7% at four-year traditional schools.

Private schools are not immune to this either. They, too, must compete for students. The more aid they can offer prospective students, the more they will attract. This puts pressure on them to accept "marginal" students and for their financial aid offices to promote federal student loans as a way to pay for their educations.

Yet, I have not seen any academic institution in any of the categories from traditional to for-profit ever suggest that the huge assets of the major academies and the lesser capabilities of the lesser endowed, should join together to help the poor students, who tried in their institutions but failed, to be rescued in any way. All of their profits are their profits and they choose to use no profits to help their failed products, their graduates, get through the loan costs needed to have little chance in life.

Maybe we should remind Academia that they are not supposed to be profit making snobs. Their mission is the education of young adults.

The federal government

As hard as it is to believe for those of us that think the federal government can do no wrong, the hoity toity constabulary running all the important agencies in Washington DC have had no problem in ripping-off millennials who managed to get their degrees. They again have had no problem bamboozling those who have put in a lot of years, taken a lot of subsidies, and still have not graduated. And, of course, the piece de resistance is that many of the products of these institutions have yet to get their first job.

It is even more clear that the federal government itself has played a major part in creating the student debt crisis. The government in Washington likes to wash itself clean of any wrong-doing but as a modern-day comedienne would say quite astutely: They're Bad, Bad, Bad!

The *don't be a plumber mentality* has not only helped fuel the idea that everyone should have a college education, it has also made it very easy to get student loans. The socialistic government of the Obama years especially encouraged every high school senior, via their guidance counselors, to fill out and submit the Free Application for Federal Student Aid (FAFSA). This assured colleges got paid for attendance regardless of the quality of the student.

The form they fill out not only goes to the Department of Education (Ed), it goes to every school for which a student has applied. The process then becomes automatic as nobody should be denied an opportunity to fail in college.

Sometime in late spring each student receives a notice of the federal financial aid they will receive based on their family's financial situation. In most cases a large part of this aid will be in the form of federal student loans, which the average family will have a very difficult time not taking. It looks like free money when it is not due for four years hence.

It cost nothing for Joey to go to college. But, when Joey graduates the debt machine begins asking to be paid. If Joey does not finish college, the debt machine comes after Joey and his family even harder because they know unless Joey gets a job, nobody will be paying back their loan.

Some say that not even a Chapter 7 bankruptcy can help if you have no money

Suppose, independent of your college life, you were reckless, and you ran up $40,000 in credit card and medical debts. The government of the US permits you to be able to get them discharged through a method called Chapter 7 bankruptcy.

Why is this? Nobody's perfect and many Americans mess up and find themselves being enticed to engage in debts which they can never repay. Often the seller of the good or service is part of the perpetration. After a while, when an individual realizes he or she cannot get out of the hole they dug for themselves, the government offers them relief.

This type of bankruptcy is known as personal bankruptcy. It is a last resort for people who are so far under, they would be candidates for the poorhouse if there was one that would take them. There is another form of bankruptcy called Chapter 13. Both Chapter 7 & Chapter 13 personal bankruptcy can eliminate overwhelming debt. With Chapter 13, you are put on a payment program so all debt will be paid for in three to five years. With Chapter 7, depending on the finding, you may find all debts discharged.

Debts may include credit card debt, bank loans, medical bills, most court judgments, and deficiencies on repossessed vehicles. Bankruptcy is not free as there is almost always a competent lawyer involved who wants to be paid. The lawyer has to figure out whether to take on a client and he or she must assure the firm can get paid. Not all lawyers will take on all cases. You will have to pay the law firm up front.

Using Chapter 7 bankruptcy, a debtor will almost always have to pay all attorney fees before your case is filed. In many cases, a friend or relative makes that payment. With Chapter 13, a large percentage is paid up front and the law firm gets paid the rest over three to five years as payments are made to all creditors.

As one might expect, an individual debtor is subjected to major harassment by debt collectors and even garnishment of wages. Those former students who are living paycheck to paycheck and have defaulted on some of their student loans are typically greeted every day with ten or more phone calls from the crack of dawn until the end of the day.

Stop Harassment / Garnishment

It is nice for an individual debtor to receive some relief from such a major disruption in their lives. For example, by law, most actions against a debtor must cease once a Chapter 7 or Chapter 13 personal bankruptcy has been filed. Creditors cannot initiate or continue lawsuits, wage garnishments, or even telephone calls demanding payments.

Keep Assets / Rebuild Credit

Debtors may be able to keep their cars, primary residence, and certain other personal belongings when filing for Chapter 7 or Chapter 13 personal bankruptcy. In Chapter 7, non-essential personal items are sold to help pay for the creditors losses.

Personal bankruptcy law firms are needed because they have the skills to help debtors retain their assets and show you what steps they must to take following the bankruptcy so that the debtor can quickly get back on their feet. They also help in rebuilding the debtor's credit immediately after the bankruptcy is resolved.

There is nothing that prevents a debtor, once free of poor-house level debt, to choose to voluntarily pay back creditors without the burden of harassment or garnishment.

Why did the Congress feel it necessary to write bankruptcy legislation? Debtors who are unable to pay their debts do not pay their debts. That is a fact. They may never get credit for anything in their lives again but there is no fallacious debtor's prison where they are kept until debt is repaid.

Nearly two centuries ago, the United States formally abolished the incarceration of people who failed to pay off debts. Bankruptcy laws actually help creditors collect when the individual has non-essential assets. However, regarding debtors, the clear purpose of Chapter 7 bankruptcy is to discharge certain debts to give an honest individual debtor a "fresh start." The debtor has no liability for discharged debts.

This form of bankruptcy can get almost all unsecured debts discharged except for alimony, spousal support, child support and… **student loan debts.** As tough as Congress is on student loans, they are easy on everyone else as debtors Only kids with the intelligence or experience to say no to college can go through bankruptcy.

Our Congress rewrote the law several years ago making student debts "bankruptcy proof." In other words, if instead of gambling on a credit card, you gambled on the value of a college education, and you lost, you cannot declare bankruptcy. *Thank You Congress.* Thank you to the hip pockets of loan shark lobbyists for giving Congress a place to live.

This means that If you have $50,000 in student loan debts, you have only two choices – to default on the loans or to repay them. It is not a good thing to default on federal student loans. Our Congress has decided former students and their parents can be bullied legally by loan debt collectors who have been given powers by our representatives that conventional debt collectors can only envy.

Yes, our kids are under the power of low-life loan sharks operating under respectable names. These bad actors got all their power by our congressional representatives. These bad guys can garnish our kids' wages without going to court. They can seize their income tax refunds and even their parents if the loan was co-signed. They can even seize part of their federal benefits such as cash welfare payments even though the cash is just enough to live.

They can also blackball them in life, so they cannot ever gain eligibility for new loans or grants. These bad actors without going to court can also put liens on their property and bank accounts.

For parents or grandparents who decided to help out Johnnie or Janie get an education, by securing a college loan, they are on the hook for life and so is their social security income. What Congress would provide a way out for credit card cheats and treats millennial college graduates like they are con artists? In my opinion, it is a Congress that should be replaced immediately

What could help? Sometimes debt negotiation works
Though there is no Chapter 7 bankruptcy relief thanks to Congress, debtors or their parents / grandparents who are on the hook for payment can seek the equivalent of a chapter 13 bankruptcy. In this type of bankruptcy, reorganization is the theme. The objective is to give the debtor time to reorganize finances and pay off debtors. Most lawyers simply tell student debt clients there is no bankruptcy relief because it is so hard to get.

The federal government's equivalent to Chapter 13 has to do with loan-modification plans. For example, one of these programs is called Pay as You Earn. Of the 45 million debtors, however, President Obama's executive order made only 1.4 million borrowers eligible.

This plan permits financially stressed student debtors to cap monthly payments at just 10% of their discretionary income and it gives them as many as 20 years to repay their loans. Unfortunately, the government is quick to turn debt over to the debt collectors, who make their money by harassing Americans.

Let me ask all Americans if this type of repayment is good for students, why would it not also be used for credit card repayments, medical bills, and the like? Can it be that too many voters would be involved?

Here is what happens when unscrupulous debt collectors and sometimes the loan servicers themselves decide to use their power against Americans.

In its #issues 2012 of American Voices, in a piece by Maureen Tkacik of Reuters titled: *The student loan crisis that can't be gotten rid of*, from August 15, 2012. In this snippet, piece, you get to see three situations where there was a clear abuse of power by the thug student loan collection industry.

> "A military veteran sharing his story with Occupy Student Debt has paid $18,000 on a $2,500 loan, and Sallie Mae claims he still owes $5,000; the husband of a social worker bankrupt and bedridden after a botched surgery tells Student Loan Justice of a $13,000 college loan balance from the 1980s that ballooned to $70,000. A grandmother subsisting on Social Security has her payments garnished to pay off a $20,000 loan balance resulting from a $3,500 loan she took out 10 years ago, before she underwent brain surgery." How is this fair? Is this what Congress actually wants?

Ms. Tkacik strengthens her case for some compassion by Congress below:

> "You have probably mentally cataloged the student loan crisis alongside all the other looming trillion-dollar crises busy imperiling civilization but also enrich the already rich."

> "But it is different from those crises in a few significant ways, starting with the fact that the entire loan business is arguably unconstitutional. You don't have to take it from me: A pre-eminent bankruptcy scholar made precisely this argument under oath before Congress."

> "In December 1975, when Congress was debating the first law that made student loans non-dischargeable in bankruptcy, University of Connecticut law professor Philip Shuchman testified that students: 'should not be singled out for special and discriminatory treatment. I have the further very literal feeling that this is almost a denial of their right to equal protection of the laws ... Nor do I think has any evidence been presented that these people, these young people just beginning their years on the whole should be singled out for special and as I view it discriminatory treatment. I suggest to you that this may at least in spirit be a denial of their right to equal protection with the virtual pole star of our constitutional ambit.' "

Chapter 3 Is the Student Loan Game Rigged?

Do Colleges and Universities have an unfair advantage?

You bet they do!

It costs Academic Institutions nothing when students come out sacked with a lifetime of debt after four to six years with no jobs. Donald Trump can recognize a rigged game better than any man in America. He can sniff them out and call them out and /or play against them and still win. He thinks the student loan game is rigged against students and it favors the universities and the government disguised as loan sharks.

Trump does not like that the game is rigged, and he has promised to fix it. The President believes that Universities must have some skin in the game for any long-term solutions to be built.

Many people are affected by the crisis and, so it is a topic at the dinner table in many homes—especially in those homes in which the student loan invoices are beginning to arrive from junior's or missy's four or five year past sojourn into campus life.

When people in the US discuss the student debt crisis, most focus on how it affects them personally. If they are not directly affected, they discuss the rapid growth in outstanding debt and its impact on the economy and the country.

They may also discuss some of the recent milestones, which are not very positive. For example, student loan debt exceeded credit card debt in 2010 and it exceeded auto loan debt in 2011. It is rapidly rising, and it passed the $1 trillion mark in 2012. It is currently at about $1.45 trillion and growing.

It is a big problem. The Wall Street Journal recently reported that More than 40% of student loan borrowers are either in default, delinquency or have postponed repaying their student loans. It is a crisis and having the federal government making over $45 billion off the backs of student borrowers in excessive interest payments does nothing to help matters.

With about 40% of students defaulting on their loan paybacks—mostly because the payments are so large, is a problem for all America. It is also a big disgrace for a country that does not want to be labeled as "Third World."

These milestones don't tell us much about the impact of all that debt on the students themselves. Seventeen and Eighteen-year-olds are making lifetime decisions even today with little counselling other than "Don't Worry! Be Happy!"

These naïve high school seniors were originally told by a friendly College Financial Aid Officer that everybody borrows, and it is a privilege to be able to attend this college with the help of the university's loan package.

Does that sound familiar. If Joe's Hot Car Lot was scamming young adults at the same rate as academia, the Justice Department would shut them down. At least Joe's Hot Cars can make it around the block. What about the kids with $50,000 in debt, no degree, and no job?

Sometimes as learned by default interviews, there was never an upfront discussion of the loan impact when it came time to repay it. As hard as it is to believe, the loans came so easy that 53% of the students when graduating, did not even know there was a payback. And we all know what payback is!

70% of all college students have borrowed and many who are already enrolled still have more to borrow before they finish their degrees and then have to pay for their college education. It is a national travesty.

America and Americans have been told by Team Obama that we are not exceptional. The way government treats the best and the brightest, who owe huge amounts of school debt, is proof that this past president and his administration were not kidding.

Meanwhile, the past president put the government in charge of huge chunks of the student loan industry. Team Obama picked up over 40 $billion a year in profits by scobbing students with high government interest rates.

No matter how immune you get to hearing about government $billions here and there, remember that a $billion is an extremely large amount of money. Even a $million is quite large. A $million is so big it gives more meaning to the word billion. It is 1000 million. Would you not like to have a $million right now?

Obama's government made the debt problem even worse for student loan debtors by taking more interest dollars than needed to sustain the program. Uncle Sam is on track to make $66 billion in profits after Uncle Obama took over the student loan program six years ago. That's why Donald Trump wants to turn the program back over to private enterprise at competitive rates.

With inflation, a college degree isn't worth much anymore. Everybody has one and the ones who should not have been admitted in the first place, are jobless and in debt up to their ears. Often, they are marginal students and they have two to six more courses to go when they drop out.

Some suggest, and I agree that certain college majors ought not ever be granted loans. Professionals with sociology and philosophy majors are not in demand. Do you know anybody who is employed as a philosopher?

Today, many students opt to continue after graduation to pursue a Master's degree. Universities, knowing the depleted value of their undergraduate degrees suggest that students take out more loans and get a Master's Degree. which may give them a better shot at a job or a promotion--maybe.

After five years or so, experience counts the most. IBM paid for my MBA, but it did not help me one way or another in my career. However, it did give me the minimum credentials to teach as a professor in a college, which I did for over thirty years part time, adjunct, and "full-time."

I know from my own family that students with graduate degrees have substantially higher debt. Law School graduates owe about $200,000 and MD Degrees owe as much as $500,000. If most undergraduate students were getting high paying jobs as in the past, the problem would not be as severe as they would be able to pay back their loans.

Bartenders, Waiters, and Short Order Cooks have a tough time handling the new government approved repayment rates for their undergraduate debt. Ironically, a college education is one of the few things in life that's value is going down, while its price is going up.

More and more parents are advising their less than valedictorian-level children to think about a trade or a less-skilled job, before committing a zillion dollars to a debt they may not be able to pay back.

Why is student debt increasing? Government under Democrat control with grants and support for postsecondary education has simply chosen not kept pace with increases in college costs. Democrats have sold out American-born College students to gain the favor of the coffee-breath liberal professors in the universities. In many ways professors talk students out of being productive members of society. Look what is happening at once prestigious universities across the country.

Government money, AKA Santa Claus, has been diverted to welfare programs and other schemes that give Democrats advantages. The one-time party of the people has forgotten completely about Americans, who are now saddled with huge debt repayment plans while foreign students who overstay their visas are getting their jobs by accepting lower wages.

Colleges are oblivious as nothing has hurt them. They make a ton of money while students and graduates scrounge for alms. This is their renaissance period as we find them going about like their product has no issues. They keep building new theatres, art museums, student centers and all kinds of amenities to attract students to make their campuses more beautiful to the eye. But, their graduates, who had one heck of a good time using all the amenities for four years, now are stuck paying the bill without a job.

Colleges and Universities need money to build, and heat these edifices to their success. So, the increasing burden of tuition financing has shifted paying for college from the federal and state governments to families using student loans as the preferred vehicle.

Meanwhile the colleges and universities are not investing in helping produce graduates capable of getting and holding jobs, Instead, the contest to become the college with the finest amenities, has pushed tuition charges through the roof.

Since grants and gifts and scholarships simply are not there anymore thanks to the Democrats in Congress, various types of loans in the "package" have become the primary vehicle today for high school students to make the jump to college.

Bankers would be fools to finance a home or an expensive car for a high school senior, who never had a loan in his life. Yet, colleges and universities are encouraged by loan sharks to provide $100,000 or more in loans to seventeen-year-olds or eighteen-year olds with no questions asked. As a professor with more than thirty years' experience, I witnessed it myself.

I know that many think that forty is the new fifty and thirty is the new twenty. Well in my observations as a professor, eighteen is the new fourteen. I was seventeen when I began college, but I know my maturity level was far more advanced than the bulk of millennials I find as students in colleges today. I graduated at 21 years of age and three weeks later I was working for IBM as a systems engineer calling on IBM computer system clients.

Tuition at King's College at the time was $450.00 per semester. Today's students take a lot more risk than I such as $16,000 per semester instead of $450.00 to be able to bask in all those great amenities. An amenity when I went to school was a desk and a classroom in which the heat worked.

Have we not been asking too much of the 44 million student borrowers who received their loans when they were "fourteen-year-olds?" Are we surprised that for the most part, they cannot handle repayment after graduation?

When I got my "package" from King's College, it included a $400 King's scholarship, a $500 in National Defense Student Loans. I also received a work study job at King's at $1.25 per hour to handle the other $50.00 for the year.

I got my degree on schedule four years later. In my second year, Pennsylvania began to give state scholarships. Tuition went up a bit and I received a State Scholarship to help cover books and incidentals.

The government no longer carries its fair share of college expenses for students, even though it gets a big increase in income tax revenue from college graduates, who are fortunate enough to get degrees and then get jobs.

Repayment begins soon after graduation

Ironically, when the first loan bill comes to the home address; first the parents, then the students are shocked that they owe so much money. Yet, each year, they signed for the new loans.

Worse than that, they become convinced at the wording of the invoice that they must pay it back. Somehow, until the risk of the student withdrawing from the institution is long past, nobody from the university finds it necessary to talk about the real cost of those loans.

In the eight years of the Obama economy and even for several years before, while "W" had a majority Democratic Congress, American family income has been flat. Many jobs were taken by illegal aliens. There was never a lot of extra anything to pay for "frills" such as education.

Therefore, moms and dads permitted their children to become college students by borrowing more to pay for college or enrolling in lower-cost colleges. So that Joey and Janey would not have to forego a dream life, mom and dad helped as much as possible but it was so easy for anybody to get a college loan, over 45 million have them today. Even smart students would ask for a little extra spending cash with the loans, so they could go to school with a little stipend and not have to work at the same time.

Jaws dropped as the tuition, the fees, and all the fun paid for by the stipend had to be paid back after graduation.

I ask myself "Why have Democrats in Congress, who theoretically love all people, not solved this lingering problem of student debt? Think about it.

If numbers could speak, what would they be saying?

In a recent policy paper that I read, student loan debt was defined as affordable if [Big IF] half of the after-tax increase in income that a student gains from obtaining a college degree is sufficient to repay that student's loans in 10 years or less. Nice try.

What if the student cannot get a job that uses his or her degree no matter what the student does? What if the student becomes a local bartender for 20 hours per week? Before we fall off the face of the earth on that notion, let's look at what the numbers might say.

Suppose the average starting salary for a bachelor's degree recipient in the humanities discipline is about $45,000 as noted by the National Association of Colleges and Employers. That figure compares with about $30,000 in average income for high-school graduates—or a $15,000 difference.

After considering taxes, the net increase for attending college and taking all the risks is about $9,000. Half of that ($4,500) is about 10% of gross income and would be enough to repay roughly $35,000 in student loans over a 10-year repayment term. This works if the policy paper thesis is operative. It is consistent with the rule of thumb that says total student loan debt at graduation should be less than the borrower's annual starting salary.

If we accept this as a definition of affordable debt, we can analyze the data from the Baccalaureate & Beyond Longitudinal Study and we would find that the percentage of bachelor's degree recipients graduating with excessive debt grew from 9.8% in 1993-94 to 14.4% in 2007-08. Let's say the percentage has continued to grow at the same rate to today. This would suggest that 16.7% of college graduates are now graduating with excessive debt. But, it sure seems like the real percentage is a lot higher—at least according to the default rate.

Why? Part of the reason is that even this percentage underestimates the bigger problem. It includes all students who graduate with a bachelor's degree—even those without any debt at all. Suppose we were to look only at students who borrowed to attend college. It appears that more than a quarter (27.2%) of them would be and in fact are graduating with excessive debt. Some statistics show the number at closer to 30%

Can an indebted student ever get back their life?

If President Obama wanted to, I believe he could have solved this problem in eight years. He could have had Team Obama analyze and fix the student debt problem rather than have it dumped on President Trump's shoulders.

Even in his trusted Cabinet and his trusty Czars, there were no MBA's. There was nobody who knew anything about capitalism and how it really works. These pompous Cretans looked down on capitalism and those trying to eke out a living in business.

They innately knew that they had all the knowledge necessary as the great elites from the SWAMP always seem to have. Nonetheless the problem is unsolved and nobody from the prior regime is talking about a great report by an expert brought in to solve the problem. There were no experts called in to help.

Looking at the reports so far in this book, you would soon find that students who graduate with excessive debt are about 10% more likely to say that it caused delays in their major life events, such a buying a home, getting married, or having children.

They are also about 20% more likely to say that their debt influenced their employment plans, causing them to take a job outside their field, to work more than they desired, or to work more than one job.

Perhaps not surprisingly, they are also more likely to say that their undergraduate education was not worth the financial cost. It is a truth that American families have yet to digest. What do universities say about that?

Nobody in the biased, corrupt press is interviewing university presidents on that subject. Why? Because the press is corrupt. But, you already knew that. The Press, the progressives, and the coffee-breath professors and administrators in our colleges and university are in cahoots. Nobody in this politically correct world would dare utter a negative word about colleges and universities.

Unfortunately, there are no similar studies that can be used to analyze excessive debt for other college degrees, such as associate degrees, certificates, and graduate or professional-school degrees. It is also not possible to evaluate the financial impact of student loan debt on students who drop out of college, even though they are four times more likely to default on their loans.

There is little financial redemption for a college dropout. Maybe that is why we find them as continual lottery players or among those restricted from casinos. Looking for their big break without having a job is a depressing, losing proposition.

What Can Be Done?

Increasing national awareness of college spending is the first step in exercising restraint. Parents understanding that colleges and universities in cahoots with loan sharks with respectable names is a big start. Being brave enough to call Congress out is part of the solution. Replacing Congress is the best option as they choose often to not hear their constituents.

It is extremely imperative that the federal government and the colleges and universities begin tracking the percentage of their students who are graduating with excessive debt each year. This information can then be used to improve student loan counseling if there actually is such a thing today in universities that want to be the most successful in marketing their schools.

Colleges must also be given better tools to limit student borrowing. Unfortunately, reality says that without federal or state insistence, these revered institutions of higher learning might choose not to use the tools designed to help students. There is the risk that a student or many students would be discouraged from enrolling and registrations would decrease.

If colleges and universities were overly willing to help students not be saddled with a huge debt with no degree or no chance of a job, what would make up for their decreased own financial opportunities? Not being able to exploit student borrowers into signing up for their huge tuition packages may be a non-starter for colleges and universities.

Colleges and universities house the smartest of the smart in the form of coffee-breath professors and those coffee-breath professors who have been promoted into the administration while still keeping their tenure rank. They have been aware of the problem for a long time but the gains from extra tuition from unqualified students have been more important than the risk of being discovered as profit opportunists.

In other words, until this point as the public is beginning to hold their feet to the fire, they have checked all of their altruistic feelings at the door. One would conclude that if the college could collect one more enrollment, a little truth bending would not be considered excessive force.

If life were fair for example, college financial aid administrators would be permitted and in fact incented to reduce federal loan limits based on the student's enrollment status and academic major.

Today, in an unfair world for students, they choose not to look at the student's prospects for success, because they may not get the acceptance and registration rate they desire. They are not evaluated as altruists but as marketing professionals. If they make minimal sales for the university, they will be fired as in any business.

Yes, doing things against the grain would be a lot of work and it might result in less revenue for the institution. Who would suffer? Students who are enrolled half-time simply should not be able to borrow the same amount as students who are enrolled full-time. But, perhaps college officials get a little back when they sell a lucrative loan package from a private lender to a student who never even should have been admitted. Who really knows?

If colleges and universities had a student-first attitude, they would also help students better understand the debt they are taking on. A student-first attitude would mean that administrators would take potential students aside and make the distinction between loans and grants clearer in their discussions, and their financial aid award letters.

Surprise, 53% of the students who get their first loan invoice did not know they owed anything? What does that's say about truth in lending? Any of the 53% should be given a full tuition refund. If the university has not taught students to know that their days in college were not free, they have failed in their mission of creating graduates capable of succeeding in the world of today.

Where is the Congress? Donald Trump is a breath of fresh air for at least he speaks about solving this problem in a business way. I believe that the new President will solve this problem because he knows how to; and he loves America and Americans more than its prestigious universities.

Let's consult with an expert

A gentleman named Mark Kantrowitz is one of the nation's leading student financial aid experts. He is the author of a number of books written for students about paying for college. His works talk about things like Filing the FAFSA, Twisdoms about Paying for College, and Secrets to Winning a Scholarship.

Mark is publisher of Cappex.com, a website that helps students achieve their college dreams, and he previously served as publisher of the FinAid, Fastweb, and Edvisors websites.

So, what?

Well, he just gave us most of the facts in this chapter.

Thank you, Mark!

Chapter 4: Solving the Student Loan Crisis and the Housing Crisis

Young people are kept down by Universities

Young and old borrowers alike owe collectively 1.45 trillion dollars of debt from their public and private student loans. With the bad economy for so long, as much as 30% of the borrowers are defaulting on their loans and this number is rising every year.

The former students simply cannot make the minimum payment. It is so bad that older students with loans are now turning 62 years of age. They get an unexpected, unwelcome surprise when their social security checks begin to be garnished by the government loan shylocks to pay off these old loans.

It is worse than you can imagine. My research discovered an 82-year old gentleman who once guaranteed a friend's loan and he is now paying 40% of his social security check to pay off the loan. He is left with $750 per month. Can this be America? Yes, it is, and in his case and many others, the principal was paid off long ago.

Many, including me, a guy who has been a professor, teaching at colleges for over 35 years, are questioning the value of a university education today. It is not a good situation when loan brokers get to collect the student cosigned debt from government's social security payments intended to sustain life.

Our major topic in this book is student debt and how to get rid of it for good. Yet, more and more experts are concluding that there is a tie-in of student loan debt and the lack of a robust housing business in the US. The homeownership rate in the United States at a 50-year low. As you might expect, it is not admissions counsellors but economists and realtors who worry about that.

The National Association of Realtors and ASA recently found that 71 percent of student loan borrowers who did not own a home cited their college loans as the main prohibitive factor. More than half indicated that they expect their student debt to delay their home purchase by five years or perhaps even more. Housing starts are a great leading indicator for the economy and when the most likely age group, twenty to forty-year-olds are not able to afford mortgage payments, something has got to change. That's why I wrote this book.

Record high home prices certainly don't help matters either. Student debt and the market aren't the only reasons millennials put off homeownership. They are not sure of a lot of things and, so they marry and have kids later in life than prior generations did. Additionally, they have seen higher unemployment rates and more sluggish wage growth than in the past. "All of that is postponing the entry point of homeownership," said Lawrence Yun, NAR chief economist.

Should we worry? Yun thinks we should. He says, "First-time buyers cause a chain reaction" in the housing market, which creates activity throughout the economy, from moving truck rentals to appliance purchases.

"That demand is central to the health of the broader real estate market," said Jonathan Spader, senior research associate at Harvard's Joint Center for Housing Studies. People are most likely to form a family and enter the housing market for the first time in their 20s or 30s. And when young adults buy their first home — often a lower-priced starter — it allows an established household to sell. "To the extent that there's weak demand at the first-time home-buyer level, it prevents existing homeowners from trading up," Spader said.

Student loan debt creates obstacles to homeownership in a few different ways. "The first is the drag on income," Spader said. It makes it tough to accumulate a down payment.

Another reason is that a student loan can make it harder to qualify for a mortgage. Lenders want all of your monthly debt obligations, including your potential mortgage payment, to make up no more than 43 percent of your monthly income. If you already pay 14 percent or more of your income toward a student loan that doesn't leave much room for a mortgage.

Another big problem on the horizon is that 11.1 percent of student loans are at least 90 days delinquent — more than any other type of consumer debt. "The impact of those defaults on their credit reports could be a barrier to homeownership in the future," Spader said. "A default is a really big deal -- it's the equivalent of a bankruptcy or a lien on your credit report,"

Asked what college hopefuls should consider as they compare schools and financial aid offers, experts suggest that it's critical to understand what your monthly loan bill will be after graduation. "Students and consumers see a number of $40,000 or $100,000, and that number is hard to wrap their heads around." The big question is "Is a $1,000 a month payment or more, every month, really going to be OK for you?"

There are a lot of possible remedies to the student loan crisis out there, which will help the homeowner crisis, but there are no guarantees. There is no silver bullet.

When people can't get jobs, and don't have the resources to pursue the dreams of a sustainable life in America, then they get to this situation where the divide between the haves and have-nots gets wider. It ripples all across our culture and economy.

That's why the overriding recommendation in this book is for the government to address the problem; find the assets to afford it, and wipe out all student debt in one big whoosh! I can assure you that there will be no housing crisis once millennials are spending-enabled. Homeowners will be everywhere if we can just get the debt noose off the backs of millennials.

Looking at the student side again, it is intuitive that students in the bottom 60% of the class have substantially lower prospects for work in their chosen field than the top 40%. One after another, many debtors in the bottom 60, are wishing they could have a do-over on that loan decision they made at 17 or 18 years of age. If so, most would never bite that bad apple again.

They now know that their huge loans; many over $100,000 are beginning to ruin their lives. Nobody, from the high-school counsellors to the College admission officers offered counselling on student debt and the negative impact it would have on the lives of so many of our young in America. Over 70% of graduates are on the hook to pay off student loans. If government, especially our Congress, was not one of the perpetrators, this would already be declared a national emergency?

Where are the good jobs that were promised by the Universities for all the money borrowed? At the same time that most graduates cannot get jobs, the jobs they do get, pay less and are often not in their field of study. The average salary of college graduates has gone down 10% in the past few years while inflation is growing at an ever-faster clip.

Moreover, 85% of college graduates from 2011 have had to swallow their pride and move home with mom and dad because they could not afford life on their own. It doesn't take a rocket scientist to call out: "Houston, we have a problem!"

The problem, to repeat, in addition to our finest representatives, is caused by coffee-breath professors, former coffee-breath professors serving as administrators, government stoolies, politicians, and progressive Democrats that like it when Americans are dependent on government.

Meanwhile the media is not saying anything bad about the universities that permit more and more foreign students into their programs. When the foreign students graduate, they are supposed to surrender their student visas, and head home. But, they do not. Moreover, the US government does not track them to make sure they do go home when their time is up in America. It makes it tough for Americans to get jobs.

Life is so good here in America, that foreign graduates often prefer to become illegal aliens, as nothing bad ever happens to an illegal alien anymore. The bad things happen to American students who graduate and get no jobs.

Guess whose jobs the foreigners on the lam take? A major source of H-1B visas (college graduates) is international students from U.S. university campuses. No corporation in America in the Obama years had any fear of hiring a foreign graduate who just became an illegal alien. They would work and still work for 50% less than a bona fide American college graduate at the same intellectual level. Colleges encourage corporations to hire their foreign students, so they could recruit more and increase profits. There is no focus on Americans.

The reason corporations hire foreigners before Americans is that they are a ready source of cheap labor. Universities not only sell their foreign national graduates to corporations, they also hire more than their fair share of professors from the foreign national community-- many of these have just received graduate degrees (PhD's) from American Universities

They fire existing faculty and replace them with younger foreign national professors willing to work for less money. I know because I was fired from Marywood University during a cost-cutting restructuring and my replacement had recently graduated from the University of Alexandria in Egypt. Marywood did not open up his employment dossier to me but what seems to be is most often what is.

Smaller Universities will even outsource the legal part of the visa work to assure the foreign applicant gets a six-year H-1B visa after graduation. This certainly does not help Americans, but it does not matter.

They will contract with immigration law firms and pay up to $10,000 or more per faculty member depending on the complexity of the case for the purpose of hiring a new faculty member who will work on the cheap. Meanwhile Americans either get fired, as in my case, or do not get hired.

Do cheap foreign speaking non-citizen faculty have any effect on the quality of education our children receive? Trying to figure out what was just said is very common in today's classrooms. "What did she say?"

It is really tough for Americans to get hired in US Universities since our Congress by law permits an unlimited number of foreign nationals to be hired as professors or staff at US Universities. Additionally, colleges also love to hire part timers at about 1/10 the pay rate of full-timers.

Buying a home without a job?

With more and more former students not being able to survive without their parents, the student debt crisis also has an impact on the student borrower's ability to ever break away. Purchasing a home is out of the question as the college loan is already bigger than the graduate's mortgage for a first home should be. As noted, this is already having a major effect on the US housing market and it will continue for years to come. Who will buy the new homes if not the young Americans, hoping to begin families.

No solution is simple. With about 30% or more former students ultimately defaulting on their loans, and many more trapped in a financial abyss from which they can never escape, Congress can certainly create a better way to help the student borrower, the housing market, and the taxpayer, all at the same time.

Considering that in the 2009 crisis, with all of the gifts from the federal government to corporations and banks that were failing, many experts have written that this money would have been better applied to the student-debt crisis. Once relieved from the staggering debt under which they suffer, you can bet millennials, all 45 million of them free from the shackles of unending debt, would be out there making America great again by purchasing one needed item after another.

I would suggest that Congress assure that in times when savings earns just a percent or two in interest, student lenders have their interest rates capped at something that is well out of the usury category. Former collegians with loans are in crisis mode in their lives while protected lenders never had it so good.

Congress can do much better for all Americans. I am a conservative and some say Republicans would not go along with a forgiveness of the student debt burden on the only Americans positioned to spend a ton of money if they had it. Shame on Republicans as many Trump loyalists have been saying for years.

Whether Congress takes it out of the fed system as it did in the $3 trillion 2009 major bailouts to corporations and banks, and nobody missed it, or it authorizes President Trump to sell some assets that are helping nobody in America, to pay for the economic restoration, the Congress has enough sheckles to forgive all student loans if they wish. If the Congress sits on its duff and wrings its hands, the next major action for those hands that I would recommend would be that they clutch the steering wheel of the family car as the one-time so and so's from such and such go back to such and such, never ever again to return to Washington.

Can you imagine the major spark in the economy if all of a sudden, millennials became the big spenders and were enabled to throw house parties in homes they never thought they would own?

The fact that Obama's government made about $43 Billion a year by charging higher than reasonable interest rates on student loans shows that solving the debt problem was never a priority during the last eight years. Let's hope Mr. Trump looks past Obama to create a system that works.

Chapter 5 What About a Progressive Loan Payback Schedule?

What if neither Trump nor Congress are in a forgiving mood?

We have already posited that the ideal solution is the 100% cancellation of the student debt obligation. Yet, nobody can make Donald Trump see what he does not see, and nobody can ask a corrupt US Congress to see things honestly. And so, people in the US who want to survive will naturally see other solutions that are much better than the alternative to nothing.

Millennials floundering in the wind, choosing to stiff the US government for their indebtedness is not a good option for America.

Without getting very complicated, besides taking away loan shylock privileges and permitting honest deserving former student candidates to file bankruptcy when overwhelmed by student loans, I would recommend putting together a progressive payback schedule.

The schedule would be like the progressive income tax schedule in reverse, based on adjusted gross income. Though we hate the tax tables, understanding them well, will help us all understand this alternate solution.

How much will I have to pay against my student debt?

Every borrower who has income from any source—a job, or government assistance, should have to pay something towards their student loan debt. If the objective were to get loan repayment dollars in, instead of sparking the economy, then nobody should pay less than 1% of their income.

Government is run by buffoons who think that if they ask for too much and the debtor opts out and pays nothing, they will have won some kind of prize, rather than have failed. Today former collegians are too often asked to pay as much as 90% of their income towards student loan debt. Naturally, this level often forces those finished with college to default on their loans just to survive. Nobody should brag about this.

Unless Congress opts on its own to rescind Chapter 7, Chapter 11, and Chapter 13, bankruptcy laws regarding student debt obligations, the first change must be to permit students already in the poorhouse, so to speak, to have the same right to file for bankruptcy as any other American with any other type of debt. Anything else is punishment. So though not on its own, Congress should do the right thing.

Standard debt payment restructuring

In addition to permitting bankruptcy as a better first option, another idea would be to permit the repayment schedule to be altered so it is affordable for the student borrower. So that student debt is not a lifetime proposition, and only those debtors in their eighties escape, those students in default or heading to default, should receive a temporary interest forgiveness.

The forgiveness should last if and until the borrower has the resources to pay again. Thus if debt is $1000 and $10.00 is paid during the year, the total debt to begin the next year would be $990.00, not $990.00 plus $85.00 = $1075. The $85.00 in this instance, of course would be the forgiven interest.

Besides forgiving interest, the payment schedule should be adjusted. However, rather than restructure debt for one student at a time in a way similar to a Chapter-13 based delinquency, a progressive schedule ought to be a standard option for any student borrower heading for default.

The objective of the program would be to get students back on track to be able to pay their debt and continue on to a productive life. We are not talking about nameless, faceless people that we are trying to help. We are talking about our children, the next crop of Americans to take over our country. Seventy percent of them are hooked on a student loan and many are overwhelmed. We need them to be participating Americans. The maximum rate of payment should be capped at 3% for the most hard-pressed borrowers. That amount would not impact life much, though it would extend the payments at 3% to 33.3 years. Additionally, all student loans should be forgiven after some age, such as 60 or 65.

When students begin to make real money, such as say, $50,000 a year, a standard progressive schedule of paybacks should be used to set the proper payment amounts. The maximum should be capped at 15% for those in default who are now doing quite well. Of course, in no instance would anybody have to pay more than the minimum monthly payment for the loan even if they could afford it.

Students who go into default often never pay anything back again--ever. So, getting something from such students is a lot better than nothing. The loss of course today is covered by taxpayer receipts.

To help pay for the program, I would also set up a fund so that any taxpayer receiving a refund can check off from $1.00 up to any higher amount on their tax forms to have part of their refund directed towards the paying down of all student loans on the books for all student debtors. We do this for campaign donations so why not for student loans?

Last time I checked, campaign donations were not in crisis. But, the student loan scenario is in a crisis. Therefore, I have other recommendations.

One of my pet peeves in all of these debt scenarios is that colleges and universities have been able to make a great profit by raising tuition to the point where they know that the government loans will pay enough for them to make a big profit or be in a position to pay huge salaries and offer far-reaching amenities to prospective students.

Do you think the following suggestion should be considered controversial?

Colleges do not suffer at all

All of this money that former students have paid and will pay over the years has already gone into the bulging coffers of universities and loan sharks across the nation, who seemingly have no skin in the game. They have already gotten paid for their "service" up front and have never been asked to look back. It's time we ask them to look back and help solve the mess they created.

They have profited by pocketing and spending the money given by their students, who may not have ever gotten a degree and who perhaps will never be able to get a job. In many cases, the problem is that the education (product of the college or university) was inadequate.

And, since the students in default, as a rule, have not been able to achieve the American dream as promised by the Admissions Counselors, the universities should contribute to a pot to make it right.

Those universities who have encouraged their foreign students to take jobs in the US ahead of American students upon graduation and those that have hired foreign faculty when Americans were available should be assessed a larger contribution for the pot.

Universities cannot be left out of the solution. Only the loan sharks and the universities have benefitted so it is a good thing to call them out and start collecting for the bum product they have put out. Yes, it should cost them until they start being more realistic and accountable, and they behave in a more American fashion, and they resolve to help Americans first.

Their admission departments and "loan" departments have actually created the problem as more than half of the graduating students are unaware that they have debt from a loan or several loans that they signed four or more years earlier. Universities are not blameless. They are a huge part of the problem. In this regard, I would ask the

Congress to enact legislation to make them part of the solution, providing a remedy such as the following:

1. Based on their student default rate, collect a fee of 3% of gross revenue to 15% (same rates as student restructured payback) that is applied to paying down all student loans. The minimum payment would be a factor of the default rate for the institution, the percentage of gross revenue, and the propensity of the institution to favor foreign students and faculty. The exact formula will need some additional work.

2. Limit the number of foreign students by law until the unemployment rate is 3% and cap the number permitted to obtain work visas after graduation to a very small / reasonable number.

3. Limit the number of H-1B visas for faculty to a very small number-- 3%. It is currently unlimited.

4. Assure the H-1B faculty member on worker visa returns to the home country after 6 years. Worker visas do not get in line for green cards or citizenship.

5. Reduce all non-University H-1B visas from 85,000 or whatever the limit is du jour by 90% until the national unemployment rate goes to 3%.

6. Since some university endowments are large because students without jobs contributed a lot of tuition dollars. The payment plan should include a certain percentage, say 3% of the total endowment each year for ten years to add to the pot to pay off student debt. To make it fair, this should be based on the default rate for the institution.

For those who do not understand the notion of an endowment, it is typically a large fund that is amassed by universities and other institutions from the kind donations / bequeathals of dedicated alumni.

The dollars in university endowments are staggering and could pay off the country's entire student debt. For example, Harvard University alone, with its 380 years' worth of alumni to hit up, boasts an endowment of $36 billion. Apple Inc.'s famously large cash hoard is just $21 billion. Yes, Harvard has more cash than Apple while students are in loan default trying to pay off their Harvard loans. Both Yale University and Stanford University's endowments are also larger than Apple's cash hoard, and Princeton University is not too far behind. Why not help some students of the past who are caught in this muddle?

Chapter 6 Forgive all Student Debt & Pay off the National Debt

Piggyback on a Trump plan to eliminate the National Debt.

America is a rich country. We have learned our lesson on student debt and on the National Debt. We have more than enough assets to wipe them both out and start fresh with a new set of rules to assure this never happens again. Only those who can afford to pay back student loans should get them, and each budget must be balanced 100%. No more US national credit card. Yes, Virginia, it is that simple.

As a candidate, now President Donald Trump promised that he would balance the national budget and pay off the national debt. By studying different thoughts on the matter, I am convinced that President Trump is right.

In no scenario am I talking about destroying Yosemite or the major National parks in the country. That would not be popular with anybody. But if we want to, we can set our debt clean in such a way that all Americans would be helped. On December 4, 2017, the president listened to Utah and gave them back about 2 million acres that Obama had stolen from them. By making selective moves such as this, we can position US and/or states assets to help America and Americans, rather than sit there doing nothing for anybody.

Keeping everything nice, a lot of minerals can produce a lot of what is needed to pay off the Student Loan Debt. Show me a reason why millennials should not be favored over monuments in which even bicycles are not permitted? Isn't that silly?

President Trump is a businessman. He has been considering selling off $16 trillion worth of U.S. government assets in order to fulfill his pledge to eliminate the national debt in eight years. He simply has to sell of a little over $1 trillion and nobody will have student debt anymore.

A senior adviser with the original Trump campaign Barry Bennett said. "How about adding another $1.3 trillion to the [national debt] repayment plans to handle student debt?" Why is that not a bad idea?

Even though the new total is $1.45 trillion, I could not agree more. Why should our next generation of intellectuals be the ones who are hurt the most by government? Once we get it paid off, we must get more selective as to who gets loans as we begin to Americanize America. We cannot ever let student loans get out of hand again.

Donald Trump is quoted as saying: "The United States government owns more real estate than anybody else, more land than anybody else, and more energy than anybody else," Bennett announced. "We can get rid of government buildings we're not using; we can extract the energy from government lands, and we can do all kinds of things to extract value from the assets that we hold."

Why should Americans be unable to begin their lives when the US is sitting on such massive assets. The bad newspapers such as the Washington Post and the New York Times want the world to think that our President is a buffoon. He is not. He is just not part of their swamp. That says it all.

In a wide-ranging interview with The Washington Post, Trump said he would get rid of the $19 trillion national debt "over a period of eight years." Of course, the debt now is approaching $21 trillion. Check out the debt clock to find out how fast our inept Congress can spend your money. http://www.usdebtclock.org/

I believe Donald Trump knows what he is talking about!

Trump has an America-First Fossil Fuel Plan.

President Trump suggests that the US takes a nice cut from opening up all US oil lands. While headlines have reported declining oil, gas, and coal prices, those declines do not deter from the fact that U.S. energy resources are valuable to our domestic economic growth. It is documented that the US now has the most energy reserves in the entire world.

The most recent government estimate of those benefits was a 2012 Congressional Budget Office (CBO) study, produced at the request of the House Budget Committee, which analyzed federal lease revenues that could be expected to arise from a proposal to open federal lands and waters to oil, gas, and coal extraction.

Unlike former president Obama, President Donald Trump is ready to bring this in right away and it will more than pay for outstanding student debt and it will also pay for a boost in social security benefits to 15% a year for the next eight years. This social security boost will help gain back for seniors what has been stolen by government supported fake CPIs. We can do it all. Why not?

In eight years, former resident Obama increased the national debt by $9.1 Trillion. When he left office the total for student debt was $1.3. Obama upset both the old and the young with his excessive spending. Not because he was so generous but because he was a miser with senior citizens providing for the first time in history, zero cost of living raises three times and once a .3 percent raise. He used a bogus cpi to stiff seniors. Can you imagine with $9.1 Trillion spent, that he did not pay off all the student debt? What can you tell me he bought for all that money?

Remember, now we need just $1.45 trillion to pay off all student debt. Instead of spending $500 billion a year on support for illegal aliens, we have the option of instituting a Pay-to Go program and a Resident Visa program that trades self-sufficiency (no freebies) for legalization or a free ticket home. If President Obama can spend $500 billion a year on illegals and he raised the debt by $9.1 Trillion on eight years, he surely could have added student loans and it would not have mattered to the debt picture.

By the way, I fully explain the cost savings that can be achieved by these new plans for illegal residents in America as well as how to pay for a plan to make seniors whole again after the government stole

438% their monthly payments. The government purposely miscalculated inflation. The whole story is in these three books

https://www.amazon.com/Boost-Social-Security-Now-Buddy/dp/194740220X/

https://www.amazon.com/Legalizing-Illegal-Aliens-Resident-Visas/dp/194740217X/

https://www.amazon.com/Pay-Go-America-First-Immigration-Fix/dp/1947402145

We need about $150 billion a year to make proper reparations to seniors who have been taken by our own government on a fake CPI approved by a willful Congress.

Look at the results from the 2015 US study below and please commit to another study ASAP:

The findings of the most recent Energy Report demonstrate that opening federal land that is currently closed-off because of statutory or administrative action, would lead to broad-based economic stimulus, including increasing GDP, employment, wages, and tax revenues. Let's look at these specifically. Who can argue if the GDP increases. It would mean the economy has finally gotten out of the dumps:

GDP increase:

- ✓ $127 billion annually for the next seven years.
- ✓ $663 billion annually in the next thirty years.
- ✓ $20.7 trillion cumulative increase in economic activity over the next thirty-seven years.

These estimates include "spillover" effects, or gains that extend from one location to another location. For example, increased oil production in the Gulf of Mexico might lead to more automobile purchases that would increase economic activity in Michigan.

Spillover effects would add an estimated $69 billion annually in the next seven years and $178 billion over thirty years.

The US is not a poor nation. We simply must stop using our resources to enrich the rich and powerful in the US and other nations. It's time to use US assets for US citizens. A proper use of oil and gas reserves will also provide a nice bump in annual job growth for thirty years in the future. Take a look at these projections that you will never see on MSNBC, CBS, NBC or ABC. Why? This is not fake news and it makes Trump's projections look good.

Jobs increase:

- ✓ 552,000 jobs annually over the next seven years.
- ✓ Roughly 2.7 million jobs annually over the next thirty years.

Jobs gains would not only be in fields directly related to oil, gas, and coal but more than 75% of the jobs would be in high-wage, high-skill employment like health care, education, professional fields, and the arts.

Wage increase:

- ✓ $32 billion increase in annual wages over the next seven years.
- ✓ $163 billion annually between seven and thirty years.
- ✓ $5.1 trillion cumulative increase over thirty-seven years.

How is all this for a plan to use US resources to help America and Americans instead of holding it just because we can. In our case, the issue is student debt but this notion from Donald Trump solves a problem with seniors in *the poor house* and an unsustainable huge national debt. How can anybody want something so good, like this, not to succeed.

It is clear that the last eight years with dependence on foreign labor has taken down the wages of Americans to near poverty levels. Recent millennials out of school are trying to get jobs and are not having much luck.

Democrats may not like this plan because it enriches regular Joe's and helps them to not become dependent on government for sustenance. Moreover, it favors American students for jobs over foreign nationals, especially, illegal foreign nationals. When everybody is doing better, the government will naturally collect more tax revenue.

Increase in tax revenue:

- ✓ $3.9 trillion increase in federal tax revenues over thirty-seven years.
- ✓ $1.9 trillion in state and local tax revenues over thirty-seven years.
- ✓ $24 billion annual federal tax revenue over the next seven years, $126 billion annually thereafter.
- ✓ $10 billion annual state and local tax revenue over the next seven years, $61 billion annually thereafter.

With increases in GDP comes increases in tax revenue. When everything is better, and people take home more salary, the treasury revenue increases substantially. Sometimes you don't have to do the math to know a winning proposition.

It ain't just me babe!

On February 5, 2013, Chris Matthews (not the political commentator from Hardball) used his fine brain to figure out a lot of things and put them in perspective for regular Americans, who do not have finance degrees. He wrote an article that he titled, *The Federal Government's*

$128 Trillion Stockpile: The Answer to Our Debt Problems? That, by the way, is more than six times the entire national debt.

We have already reviewed much of this material as the proof that the US can do quite well by using our own resources to treat all of our citizens well. I am in synch with Matthews' conclusions as noted in the prior segment of this chapter. That given, Chris has had a lot of other good stuff to say to help America and Americans. It ain't just me saying it babe!

As a regular human being who happens to have an MBA in Accounting and Finance, I have watched the debate over federal government deficits and debt, which has consumed Washington for some time.

Logic dictates that the financial world will explode if the US keeps spending excessively like drunken sailors. Yet for eight years despite prediction after prediction, the US is still at the top of the globe? Despite what the doomsayers say, we can probably keep spending like drunken sailors and not pay the price, because our asset base is so huge. That means we can wipe out Student loan debt, make seniors whole with eight years of 15% raises as reparations, and we can pay off the national debt. And, why shouldn't we?

Moreover, just about every country invests in the US and they consider their dollars safe. With all of our assets, dollar investments in America ae safe. Once we get all the crap paid off, we can go ahead and create better fiscal policies and keep it clean from hereon in. Nothing has yet to explode though President Obama guided America through eight years in which whatever Lola wanted, Lola got.

Republicans were scared cats and never said no to Lola and the cowards never said no to Obama. Democrats loved Lola so much that even though they never saw the back of her hand as she stuck it out for one handout after another, they were compelled to reach way into the bowels of the treasury department to give her more and more.

Now, all of a sudden, these same *give-away Charlie's* in Congress who love giving handouts to illegal aliens, cannot find the cash to boost social security benefits to remove seniors from the poverty rolls and they can't find enough good heartedness to solve the student debt crisis. What can Congress do?

Yes, instead of helping students riffled with debt, they punished recent college graduates with usurious interest rates and no opportunity to discharge debt when bankrupt, rather than giving them the helping hand they need to become successful Americans.

Yet, still we are here, a stable country despite being $20 trillion dollar in debt—at least supposedly. Despite the doom and gloom, most regular people have yet to notice a change with all the debt supposedly getting ready to finish off America. Where are the death blows? They are not here, and they are not coming.

Has all this debt hurt us, and if so, how? It makes one think that it may all be a ruse. Have you ever seen a list of *to whom* we owe all the debt? Why are they not clamoring for an immediate payoff if things are so bad?

How disingenuous for Democrats, the biggest spenders in town to complain that giving Americans a tax break in December 2017 would hurt the National Debt Situation. For eight years, Obama and company were able to jack up the national debt at will and he did not even have to explain why! What can we believe anymore?

We know that we cannot believe the corrupt press and now we can't believe the corrupt Democrats who wanted us to believe we could exist on continuing resolutions and no budget for all the Obama years.

Now, all of a sudden, we need a tight budget. Excuse me? Who is kidding whom? If Congress wanted to give student loan borrowers a break and wipe out all student debt and help seniors by doubling seniors' social security checks, would any of us have noticed the strain on our treasury. I think not. So, why not just do it to help America and Americans while we get our house in order.

Now we are somehow to believe that if the Republicans get their new tax reform and a revamped IRS system, we will suffer. In fact, it won't help, and it won't hurt the stability of the nation at all; but it sure will help all those who get a nice tax cut…and it is about time.

The impact on the national debt will not matter an iota just as it has not mattered in the best or the worst of Obama times. So, why bother fretting about it? Of course, for middle income Americans, the impact of the tax cut and the post-card return form will be substantial.

The original arguments for the most part all have been focused on taxes and spending. One aspect, however, of the debate of American creditworthiness that never was discussed is what Donald Trump saw when he looked into the eyes of the huge federal government assets.

If the US is in debt (to whom) so much, then why do we not know who the people are that we owe such amounts to. What are their names?

Should not the assets of a big borrower like the USA be one of the main factors in determining the wisdom of whether the US has a right to continue to borrow and borrow and borrow?

Nonetheless, despite logic well proven in the past, when the US government's debt burden is the topic of conversation, the press has always been willing to remove it from the daily conversation entirely. What do they know that we do not know? Why do they root against regular normal Americans?

There is a recent report from the Institute for Energy Research (IER) that makes more claims about America's prosperity in the future than Donald J. Trump, himself has made. It makes some startling claims about how much U.S. taxpayers own in real assets, through the authority of the government. According to the report, the U.S. government (the people) owns:

- ✓ More than 900,000 separate real assets covering more than 3 billion sq. ft.
- ✓ Mineral rights, on and offshore, covering 2.515 billion acres of land, more than the total surface land in Canada
- ✓ 45,190 underutilized buildings, the operating costs of which are $1.66 billion annually
- ✓ Oil and gas resources on and offshore worth $128 trillion, roughly eight times the national debt of the country [at the time of this report]

Unlike this opinion piece by a guy who loves America [the other Chris Matthews] and thinks all student borrowers are being ripped off, the author of these statistics, IER, is a think tank that advocates for deregulation in the energy industry.

Do we trust the government to tell us the truth?

It is a given that any estimate of oil and mineral wealth in unexplored areas is highly speculative. However, none of these research firms want to fail by a factor of 100%.

So, even if the true figure is half what the IER estimates, the fact that the federal government owns property worth well in excess of its total debt is instructive in our current debate about government borrowing. Why would anybody loan the US a buck if the best it could get back was just seventy-five cents?

They loan to the US because we have tons of natural assets.

Regular people have no idea about what the Federal Government's asset total might amount to. Those who do not want a clean slate are motivated to claim we are in trouble. Yet, our assets are innumerable.

The problem is that America's least honest and most pompous and least intelligent people run the government. Yes, I am talking about our Congress who collectively and individually are incompetent, and they are fine in their ineptness.

The non-government, aka US citizens as a group, own much more than just land and the minerals and the oil beneath it. The non-government under the auspices of the federal government also has a very sizable stash of gold., and certainly other stashes of valuable items that it would prefer were not discussed generally.

In fact, at oz., the US has the largest holdings of gold in the world. And, in case you have not noticed, gold is a favorite among investors who have a deep concern about the debasement of government currencies in this era of worldwide, aggressive monetary stimulus.

When the original article was written, the going rate of $1,660 per ounce was easy to be gained on a trade. It is actually a bit less right now. At that rate, the US stash is worth nearly $442 billion. Even that would pay for 1/3 of the student debt owed by mostly the millennials in our nation.

Those of us that know well the meaning of the phrase, "old fart," know that ever since Richard Nixon broke the link between the dollar and gold in 1971, there's has been no official justification for America's sitting on all the gold in Fort Knox. Why not split it up among the citizens or pay off 1/3 of all student loans?

At least some of it could easily be used to pay down the general debt or put toward neglected projects like infrastructure. Of course, if instructed, the US treasury could also use this stash to reduce student debt liability. After all, the debtors are your children and mine.

Ironically, on the US books as a major asset is the portion of the $1.45 trillion dollars that student loan borrowers owe—about a cool $1trillion.

Why not just cancel that and let's all start over? Think about it?

Most Americans would admit that there is a downside to selling off US assets and the sell-off might put major policy objectives at risk. But, it is about time we evaluated these policy objectives against the need to keep our brightest from pulling out of the economy because they can no longer afford their student debt. We can do better.

As noted, it is amazing for many that the federal government still holds on to so much gold. Why? With gold prices so high, it probably makes sense to unload at least some of it for the support of the country. But, we would need to make sure that our untrustworthy Congress did not squander it.

The irony in checking out US assets is it must have something to do with why the whole world is still eager to lend the U.S. money. Despite all the doom and gloom from the corrupt media, the US has so many obvious assets that our country is still the most credit worthy nation in the world. We are still a very rich country in both productive capacity and industrial and natural resources. We should not have our brightest and youngest adults trapped in a debtor's prison scenario until they grow old.

The financial crises and demographic shifts that have caused our budget problems are either temporary effects or problems that could be solved by a mature discussion about priorities.

If we could sell off just a bit of our hard assets, we could free our most worthwhile assets, the minds of our newest generation to be able to advance their lives positively and help out our country in so doing.

Chapter 7 Should We Fret About the Debt?

Why has the National Debt not crushed us?

In trying to get a grip on why we actually can choose to forgive the entire student debt load and give a 15% a year boost to social security recipients, Mike Norman has written a nice piece that he titles The National Debt: Why Fret Over Something That Doesn't Exist? I asked Mike if I could reprint his article in this book. Here it is below:

The National Debt: Why Fret Over Something That Doesn't Exist?
By
MIKE NORMAN
OCT 25, 2016 | 1:00 PM EDT

> The public is lied to when it comes to the so-called national debt. They're clueless about it, as are most, if not all, of our lawmakers.
>
> First off, there is no debt. The debt is dollars. The government spent $20 trillion more than it took away in taxes over the last 240 years, and those dollars, held by the non-government, comprise a big portion of the non-government's wealth. Nothing is "owed." It's owned, by us, the people.
>
> Second, there is nothing to pay back. The money was paid, ended up in someone's bank account and now it's being held in the form of Treasuries.

What's a Treasury? A Treasury is a dollar, the only difference being it's a dollar with a term (duration) and a coupon (interest payment).

Why would people hold dollars in the form of Treasuries? To earn some interest, that's all. It's like saying, why would you put your money in a savings account as opposed to a checking account? Same reason, to earn interest. If you want it back in your checking account, you tell your bank and it switches it back from your savings account to your checking account.

That's how it works with the government, too. It "pays back" holders of Treasuries all the time. That's called a redemption and when Treasuries are redeemed the government simply instructs its bank, the Fed, to take back the securities and credit the individual's (or firm's or foreign government's or whoever's) bank account and, voila, it happens. Paid back.

In fact, it happens so regularly and on such a big scale that it will totally blow your mind.

I am about to give you some numbers. Mind you, these are not numbers I made up or to which had some kind of top-secret access. Nor is this inside information that I am exposing.

Rather, these are publicly available figures that you can get—free—right off the U.S. Treasury Department's website.

The resource is called the Daily Treasury Statement and it's really a fascinating document. It is posted daily on the Treasury's website and it's literally like looking at the checkbook of the federal government. Just like your checkbook, it has all the deposits and all the withdrawals, among other things.

You can see everything. Every line item of spending (withdrawals) and every item of revenue (deposits) that runs through the government's accounts daily, monthly and yearly. Table III below:

On this document there is a table -- Table III-A -- that gives all the redemptions of bills, notes, bonds and other securities the government redeems (pays back) every day, month and year.

If you go to the last statement of the fiscal year, Sept. 30, and you scroll down to that table I just gave you, Table III-A, you will see the government redeemed (paid back) $94.2 trillion in one year! I put a screenshot below

Please note: All figures on the daily Treasury statement are in millions, so don't come back to me and say it was only $94.2 million. It's $94.2 million, million. That's $94.2 Trillion. See the image below.

Daily Treasury Statement Shown on Following Page:

[You can see charts it better in the original article at the following URL

https://realmoney.thestreet.com/articles/10/25/2016/national-debt-why-fret-over-something-doesnt-exist]

```
                          DAILY TREASURY STATEMENT                          PAGE: 4
              Cash and debt operations of the United States Treasury
                             Friday, September 30, 2016
                  (Detail, rounded in millions, may not add to totals)
```

TABLE III-A Public Debt Transactions

Issues	Today	This month to date	Fiscal year to date
Marketable:			
Bills:			
Regular Series	$ 0	$ 593,009	$ 5,700,876
Cash Management Series	0	0	95,032
Notes	118,827	162,827	2,855,965
Bonds	0	12,000	189,114
Inflation-Protected Securities Increment	-18	-1,707	10,700
Federal Financing Bank	0	0	2,685
Nonmarketable:			
United States Savings Securities:			
Cash Issue Price	3	77	899
Interest Increment	3	449	5,500
Government Account Series	411,005	7,771,840	87,217,752
Hope Bonds	0	0	0
Domestic Series	0	0	0
Foreign Series	0	0	0
State and Local Series	96	11,807	99,366
Other	1,042	23,265	270,694
Total Issues	$ 530,959	$ 8,573,571	$ 95,648,594

(Stated at face value except for savings and retirement plan securities which are stated at current redemption values.)

Redemptions	Today	This month to date	Fiscal year to date
Marketable:			
Bills	$ 0	$ 578,994	$ 5,506,942
Notes	94,603	125,603	1,705,765
Bonds	0	0	29,837
Federal Financing Bank	0	0	1,976
Nonmarketable:			
United States Savings Securities	39	1,018	11,301
Government Account Series	394,653	7,776,014	86,627,213
Hope Bonds	0	0	494
Domestic Series	0	0	0
Foreign Series	0	0	0
State and Local Series	67	5,542	68,270
Other	1,042	23,251	270,959
Total Redemptions	$ 490,404	$ 8,510,422	$ 94,225,757
Net Change in Public Debt Outstanding	$ 40,554	$ 63,149	$ 1,422,827

Ninety-four point two trillion! In a single year. And nobody knew about this. Furthermore, the world didn't fall apart, the dollar didn't collapse, interest rates didn't spike, we had no inflation and everything was fine.

There is the proof, right in front of our noses, that the debt is meaningless. It's just a bunch of bookkeeping entries. Keystrokes. It's time we stop fretting over this. People need to educate themselves about what this debt is and how they are being manipulated and propagandized about it.

The debt is not a bad thing, it is an asset of the non-government; however, ignorant, cynical, corrupt, dogmatic and self-serving groups like the Pete Peterson Foundation and organizations like Fix the Debt are in the business of keeping Americans misinformed and getting them to act against their own interests. These groups are bad and need to be stopped.

There is no debt! Please share.

Chapter Conclusions

I have no particular love for millennials but like it or not, they are Americans and they are our direct progeny. We have no other. What Congressional policy and corrupt student lending practices have done to them is a sin for sure against them and all of America. We need to end it now.

I have proven ten-times over that we can both afford it and help all of America at the same time. By energizing a group of our forgotten young adults, our economy can make Donald Trump's 3.3% GDP increase look like chump change.

Either Congress does this for us or we get a new Congress. It is that simple. We the People!

Chapter 8 Congress Treats Student Borrowers Poorly

It's like it's your kids; not their kids!

One would think we either elected buffoons or people who simply do not care about u--or both.

If we did not elect them, that is what we got anyway. There ought to be enough money in the federal budget to hire experts. Donald Trump and every other successful business mogul runs their businesses with experts to make a buck. Our Congress is clearly not made of experts.

Nobody does it alone and nobody hires the second team to do the job. How could our legislators be as ambivalent on something as simple as the interest rates for student loans? They are harlequins, I regret to say, and their time has come. Smart Americans must send them home for good and find other smart Americans to take their places.

History of student loan interest rates

Let's take a look at the tumultuous history of student loan interest rates. At best it is characterized by bipartisan indecision, delayed legislation and temporary solutions. Congress gets a solid "F" grade for this performance. At worst, the government hired workers with the lowest IQ's to figure this out.

Understanding the events is key to knowing Congress's thinking on interest rates' current trajectory. Here's a quick summary of the last 20 years in student loans. This information was gleaned from the New America Foundation.

1992-93: (6.94%) Variable interest rates are introduced for federal student loans.

1993-94: (6.22%) Congress creates the direct loan program to gradually eliminate the need for bank loans.

1994-95: (7.43%) The variable rate maximum drops from 9% to 8.25%.

1998-99: (7.46%) The interest rate change set to begin in 1998 is postponed another five years. C

2001-02: (5.99%) The scheduled 2003 alterations become a topic of debate. Student advocates defend the change.

2002-03: (4.06%) The 1993 rate change is canceled. The current variable rate remains in place. In 2006, loans will begin to carry a 6.8% fixed interest rate.

2004-05: (3.77%)

2005-06: (5.3%) With the 6.8% fixed rate in place, Congress launches a campaign pledge to cut student loan interest rates in half.

2007-08: (6.8%) Making good on the pledge, Congress passes a bill for a temporary 4 yr. interest rate reduction.

2008-09: (6% for Subsidized Stafford, 6.8% for other loans)

2010-11: (4.5% for Subsidized Stafford, 6.8% of other loans) Third phase of rate cuts, Congress eliminates the bank-based federal student loan program.

2011-12: (3.4% for subsidized Stafford, 6.8% for other loans) The fourth and final phase of temporary rate cut.

2012-13: (6.8%) The 2007 rate reduction expires on July 1, 2012 and rates revert to 6.8%.

Apr. 27, 2012: The House passes bill to extend the 3.4% interest rate.

2015-2016: (4.29%)

2016-2017: (3.76%)

2017-2018: (4.45%)

Follow the bouncing ball...

One thing is for sure, Uncle Sam positioned the government to make a killing on student loans. Uncle Sam is the bad guy here just as Uncle Obama was when he took over the student loan program to help finance Obamacare.

Would you believe the government is not your friend?

The secret behind the curtain is a dirty secret. The federal government does not want any of us to know that it makes an enormous profit under the federal student-loan system — an estimated $433 billion over the next 10 years. Some critics of student loans say that it's nothing more than a boondoggle paid for by super-inflated tuition costs and driven by the government-sponsored predatory lending system.

A second little secret is that the Department of Education (ED) actually profits if you default on your loans. This is because it makes money on students that default. It's estimated that the ED collects an average of 100% of the principal on these loans, plus an extra 20% in fees and payments.

Assigning student graduates to debtor's prison

Raising the loan rates as the federal government did in mid-year 2012 for Stafford Loans helped about as much as putting all the student debt laggards, many from our own families, into a debtor's prison. This is not part of my solution.

About seven million students had enjoyed "reduced rate" Stafford loans to help them get through college. The interest rate on these loans was scheduled to double on July 1, 2012. It was heading from 3.4 percent to 6.8 percent unless Congress acted. Congress, a group who have no time for America while being paid by Americans let the rates go up.

The House had already passed the necessary legislation to do so and the Senate was planning a similar action. This would raise costs by an average of $1,000 each, according to the White House. While many students were already in default, a thousand dollar increase surely was not expected to help them pay their loan off any quicker.

When students default, it is not good. In some cases, they ruin their lives, and it costs us all. Ask yourself why interest rates are so high on student loans. They are higher than mortgages. How is that? Ask Congress!

Who determines that interest rate? Who pockets it? The government scobs our kids at a high rate while offering less than one percent on deposits. How is that fair? To repeat, Obama's increase still brings in over $45 billion a year in revenue from students who were told they could borrow to get ahead in life. Now, millions are stuck in a rut.

Students with a debt of $100,000 or more, and there are more and more and more of them, face payments well over $1,000 per month. That is tough to pay when you are unemployed. It is tough to pay if you are on Social Security. That is why over 8 million student borrowers have already defaulted and more default every day. Check out why the US Congress introduced bankruptcy laws in the first place.

For your edification, it helps to know that somebody is making a killing on this interest and it is not you or me. The National Student Loan Debt Clock raises 2,726 dollars per second according to Market Watch.

When I paid off my National Defense Student Loan (NDSL) in the 1970's, my payments were just over $10.00 per month. I paid it off as soon as I could as it was just an annoyance. I also had a PA State low-interest loan and its payments were closer to $25.00 per month. It took a little longer to pay this off but by the time I was married at 27 years old, all of my student loan debts were paid.

This is not possible today. Back then, the government was not interested in sending young men and women into debtor's prison or making them dependents of government for life.

Today's students are looking at big payments for a long, long time and while they are making those payments, they are postponing serious relationships, postponing starting a family, and postponing buying a new home. Ironically, millennials fail to see a connection between their experiences and the US government's philosophies. Yet the connection is there.

Millennials simply cannot afford the big loans and the more oppressive the government makes payback terms, the more likely student borrowers simply give-up. They just drop out; stop paying; and stop answering the phone. That surely does not help the US taxpayers or those who build homes for a living. Of course, we can throw all these young "bums" in jail?

Can Mighty Mouse save us all? Can Mighty Mouse save any of us? "Here I come to save the day… that means that Mighty Mouse is on his way!" Don't count on it but the Mighty Obama did take a swipe at the problem and it has been recorded.

On Oct. 26, 2011 President Obama decided to save the world—again. He came out with a new initiative that would allow student borrowers to cap their loan repayments at 10 percent of their discretionary income starting sometime in 2012. The consequence of Obama's directive was that the effective date was two years earlier than the same act that was passed by Congress. Obama likes doing things without Congress. BHO took credit for something already underway.

In October 2011, ABC reported that Obama said: "We can't wait for Congress to do its job. So, where they won't act, I will." Upon inspection, unfortunately, as well intentioned as it might have been, the Obama plan did not help those who already had student loans (pre-2008) and had graduated or had left school. In other words, most of the students with the problem were not part of this solution. But, it was good press.

I have a better plan than Obama's for potential borrowers as you will see when you work through this book. You will see that this is a solution for those student borrowers and their parents who are already stuck in the mire. There are about 45 million student borrowers, so chances are you know somebody who is stuck.

Chapter 9 Should I Go to College?

It depends is the best answer.

This was never a tough question in the past. The answer was always "YES." It is a tough question to answer nowadays. Unless you are convinced that you can be at a minimum in the top 25% of your class, and you are willing to work unbelievably hard to assure your class rank, you are better off trying to get a job right now and forego college temporarily. That is just an opinion.

From the 1960s on, there never was a question even if it were asked. "Everyone needs to go to college, right? Right." If you want any sort of job today – up to and including clerking or being an executive assistant – for years you're told you need a college degree. But does it always work out? Less and less!

And, so, some people believe that the whole idea that everyone needs to go to college is nothing more than ill-founded social engineering much the same as the idea in the early 2000s that everyone should own a house. Did you ever hear of the subprime housing crisis? Of course, you did!

Where do we go from here?

How does the thinking that right or wrong you must go to college work out in reality? Most young people who buy into this idea do not have enough money to pay today's super-inflated college costs. There is a great solution at hand. They borrow the money.

They are not credit worthy enough to buy a moped, certainly not a motorcycle, a car or a small home. But, somehow, they can secure a loan of equal or more value that without a big job after graduation, they can never pay back.

Why does any lender take on such a risk? Because government secures the loan for them even if the student has no chance in college.

This year's college students graduated owing an average of around $39,000 only to discover that due to the poor job market they have less of a chance than ever of actually getting a good job in a field commensurate with their degrees. Too bad!

The sellers of the stuff they bought, the coffee breath professors and the big shots in academia never agree for the student borrower to take out the big eraser and wipe their signatures off the loan documents. The kids are in it forever.

If I had a say

Since seventeen-year-olds operate as the new fourteen-year-olds today as I see it, I would suggest that nobody gets a student loan until they are the new seventeen, which would be twenty-one. Everybody once released from college with or without a degree and almost always with a huge debt package, are looking to achieve a good-life today. Too late! Unless the fourteen-year-old in you at seventeen made the right loan decisions, you are done unless Congress steps up and does something.

If it became a law, all decisions by students hoping for a college degree could be made with cash. No problem. Loans would be outlawed for college degrees in my world until you were twenty-one. You could use your cash at any age and enroll. It's on the cash provider.

However, for those with no cash, and no relative providing cash as a sponsor—until they were from birth to twenty-one years-of-age, there would be no loans for them to attend any college. Once they hit twenty-one, the new seventeen, they would be granted student loan privileges.

By that time, when they reach twenty-one, hopefully, these affected millennials would have engaged in several jobs and would understand better what life is all about.

I would suggest the following to students contemplating college today as seventeen-year-olds operating as fourteen-year-olds: Go home. Don't ruin your life. Male or female, see first if you like being an artisan, a wood craftsman, a plumber, or an electrician, before you bet on the cum-line on making it big by investing $25,000 or more for year one of a college career that today is very iffy.

Unless somebody is handling your tuition other than you or a loan, "Do not go to college full-time. You are the only one taking the risk that it will help you in the future. If it does not help you; you may be strangled by debt. If you do not graduate or others beat you big time in the class-rank area, you will suffer all your life for the mistake of choosing college over a career in another field that does not require a degree."

Worse than that at $25,000 per year, when you find out what you want to pursue in life, it will be much less easy to achieve if you have $100,000 of debt strapped to your back. Everybody will see it. That's just the way it is.

I would suggest taking a few college courses at a time in your spare time and in the summer. Don't take English unless that is your love. Read a lot and write a lot. Get enrolled into a course in the discipline you might choose to follow. See if you can be an engineer. See if you can be a computer technician. See if you can be a chemist.

Do not take easy courses that work towards your credit requirement as you may find you don't want to be an Oceanographer but instead a diver and what a shame to have all that student debt when being a diver does not cost quite so much!

Until you absolutely must, know that so many others are swamped today by student loan debt. Mostly it is unnecessary if you don't set a four-year degree plan in motion. Do not take out any student loans. Ever! Save your life so you can be free.

What does Sue think?

When a reader named Sue commented on the ABC report of Obama's initiative on their News site, she offered the best advice I have seen in a long time to assure new students that are not now swamped by student debt, to avoid ever getting into the big student borrowing hole.

Sue responded with tremendous insight into the real problem today with student loans—the 800-pound gorilla in the room that nobody wants to talk about in an honest way.

In Sue's words: "I actually don't believe that we should put a college education in everyone's hands and think that line of thinking is part of the problem with education in this country." Sue continues:

"For decades we've restructured our elementary and high school systems to become one-size-fits-all and college is quickly going that route too. But the reality is that not everyone fits the mold. Not everyone is cut out for an office job and not everyone is cut out for construction.

"In some communities, we are now seeing a return to skills training in high schools, where kids can graduate from high school with a two-year business degree from the local community college and a cosmetology license, or a mechanics license as well as their high school diploma.

"These are kids who can go right from high school into the work force with the training they need, start working (or start their own business from their parent's garage). They won't be saddled with student loans."

"The President's program [Obama era] of encouraging students to go into debt (sorry, but a student loan is a debt) to get an education is backwards – and in the end, not everyone needs a college education to move the country forward. They simply need to be trained to do what they want to do, and preferably, they should learn it in high school." [Preferably, they should not have to be on the verge of lifetime bankruptcy when they understand their choice of professions in life.]

Bring back Kuder aptitude tests in high school

Sue did not say this but surely, she was thinking about it. We need better aptitude tests and attitude tests s that we do not overly respect a college education.

Let's bring back the Kuder tests to check aptitude in high school and stop the insistence that everybody needs to complete their life by having gone to some college someplace at some time. Unless you can afford the $100,000 and are willing to accept nothing in return, stay away from College scene unless again, you are convinced that you will be in the top 25%-33%.

Sue has a head on her shoulders for sure.

Who in a debtor's prison ever has earned enough to gain their freedom? More and more student borrowers, who are already in de facto debtor's prisons see the invisible bars, and choose to escape in the only way they know how. They stop paying even a dime towards their student debt and they stop answering their phone.

They see their student debt as hopeless. After a few reprieves, a few thousand 8 AM phone calls that wake-up mom and dad, several forbearances, with their debt climbing through the roof, they give up and call it quits. For a while before the end, they believe they are paying for the right to remain out of default, in much the same way they would if the dollars were borrowed from a loan shark. Then they find that the merely paid to get a forbearance and none of the debt is paid. Yes, the government loan sharks take all these payments, and none apply towards the loan. How does that help America's young adults. It makes them want to quit paying for sure.

Wen their total debt balance goes up as they send checks thinking they are paying against their debt, they finally reach a point where the alternative is a better alternative. Why bother? They default on their loans.

Eight to nine million and growing have defaulted so far and they ruined their big opportunities in life. But, paying the most they could for years without decreasing the principle was ruining their little opportunities.

The system is unfair and once smart student borrowers know the game is rigged against them, and that they cannot get ahead, and they cannot change the system, they are smart enough to quit trying. After all they are products of the American higher education system. They know they are being ripped off.

Some want the "deadbeats" to suffer

There are those successful and somewhat lucky graduates who are not suffering from the pain of this huge debt since they have the means or the jobs to pay off their loans. I have read their comments. They do not want those less fortunate to get a break, especially if they perceive they will be paying for it or if their kids struggled with it and succeeded.

Though they are in the minority, many of them are indignant that the others, not so lucky should get a small break, and surely not a big break. They have little compassion for those who do not pay their bill even if they have no job and no means of support. If they gave it little thought, they would agree that such deadbeat borrowers should be put in debtor's prison to teach them a lesson.

They resent the fact that they had to pay off their debts on their own in order to move ahead. This is understandable to an extent but what do they want the guy or gal who they beat out for the only job in town to do?

From the Internet chatter on student loans, many that are doing well do not think that their university peers should even ask taxpayers to help them pay off their loans as it would be unfair to those, such as the fortunate with jobs, who are paying or who have paid their loans off on time.

I agree with their outrage, but the reality separates itself from their outrage. This is surely understandable, and I would have do have reservations about forgiving all of these debts. Yet, I believe it is best for America is we forgive them and start the system over the right way.

It would be a good idea for those in default, those about to default, and those who ultimately will have to pay for the default to consider making the debt able to be paid without major pain. Nobody gains when the debt is rendered uncollectible and the once hopeful student's life is basically ruined for good.

None of us will ever get in line to give what is not needed to the poor, but most will help as much as we can. I like to say that I will always help the helpless, but I do not want to help make anybody helpless. Giving student loan relief is an exception.

It won't make anybody helpless. It is help that can make people productive for the first times in their lives in some cases. It is good for America. From talking to the parents of students in default, I can assure you that no parent, who in good faith sent their children to higher education institutions that promised the world, expected less of a life in return.

Nobody expected the world in a basket either. However, nobody expected a life of misery after gaining their coveted degree. Meanwhile, the university and the other loan sharks including the US government long ago—all of them—have cashed the checks even though the granted degree in many cases is worthless to this graduate. Perhaps that degree is worthless to most graduates in that particular degree program. But, only the student borrower who got nothing out of it, is on the hook.

Do not trust admissions counsellors

As a thought that we have introduced earlier in this book, it helps to recognize that at the bottom of the student debt issue today is that colleges and universities oversold their product. What college today is suffering because none of their students were able to get jobs. When you answer that question, I might feel compelled to scream out "I rest my case!"

The dike is still leaking as colleges are still able to do this with impunity. There are no laws that compel a college not to overpromise. Why not? You find no big stories about colleges being punished for not doing a good job in training our children to excel and perhaps more importantly, to be able to so think for themselves. Isn't that the job of colleges and universities? If not, what is their job? I

US colleges and universities should be punished by having to help their student graduates with their loan repayments. Don't you think that alone would help solve the student loan crisis in the future?

Not learning from their mistakes, universities create a never-ending cycle of students heading for the debtor's prison. These one-time students often get no chance at stopping for a brief respite to have a life, a house, a husband, or a child.

Without assurances of a top-class rank, no sane parent, properly advised by a school or a compassionate government, would have encouraged their children to take out huge school loans approaching a hundred thousand dollars after four or five years unless they knew something good was going to happen. They believed what was said.

In the end, they see their children with a worthless education and a worthless piece of paper to hang on the wall. Now that the results are in, and there are almost nine million loan defaults equaling nine million ruined lives, what sane parents should consider signing up their next child today with the same risk of ruining his or her life.

Only the colleges and universities benefit and it is time that they get called on it. It is far better to be unemployed without a huge debt than to be unemployed and be heading to the veritable debtor's prison until the loan is paid off.

Our Congress does not permit bankruptcy as a solution for young people who cannot pay their student debts. But, if they had paid for their degrees on high interest credit cards, they may actually be permitted bankruptcy relief.

Many parents expected and some still believe that the very act of going to college should result in guaranteed success. The success would include a good job for the graduate and thus there would be a means of paying for the education even if the interest rates were unfair.

Even more importantly, paying off the loan is looked upon as a side show on the ladder of success. Having a fine job that is good enough to provide the means to buy a home and have a better life—that is looked on as the piece d' resistance! For today's older kids, neither are achievable.

Today, unfortunately, as parents have found, the verdict is in. Unless you are in the top 25% of your class, those dreams are unlikely to materialize. Worse than that; those parents who were duped by the admissions counselors in the fancy suits witnessed their children being set up for a life of future miserableness that might just as well be a debtor's prison. I am afraid it is that bad.

Go to the Internet and type in student loan repayments and you can see the despair and the disappointment expressed by the victims of the student loan charade created and continually espoused by our Congress. If you think the credit card issue with young people is bad, consider that Congress decided that with student loans, your children can get no relief at all—ever.

Shall we say the loan sharks / lobbyists and their accomplices in the colleges and universities convinced Congress to act in such a way that does not help students who are merely trying to better themselves? I think you can win a bet on that one. Ask Congress why they do not help today's most academically talented poor?

The irony is that colleges and universities are mum about the problem as if they have no culpability at all. These institutions have become in many ways like the bad businesses listed by the Better Business Bureau.

Ironically, in recent years, as a recruiting tool, colleges and universities, especially those that operate mostly online, have found a need to register with the Better Business Bureau. Moreover, they use their listing to prove their worthiness to students. The truth is missing from their work.

Better Business Bureau certified

For the Better Business Bureau, legitimate proof of success for a college or university to produce is simply that they actually do bestow degrees. Degrees are simply pieces of paper even if somebody does not respect the supposed meaning of the paper.

The degree of course is intended to represent the end of a major higher educational process that provides the knowledge for one to be successful in their area of study. When presented in the form of a sheepskin or a rolled piece of paper, for the BBB, that is proof positive that the university is not in a scam business. What do the students who have been scammed by colleges and still are not working think of that premise?

When I wrote an article about this debtor's phenomenon in 2012, I was misinformed. I wrote this: "But, does it really provide the proper proof? Are the universities of today, where 85% of American graduates in 2011 were so inadequately prepared for life that they had to go back home for sustenance, really worthy of being heralded by the Better Business Bureau as bastions of opportunity."

My apologies to those who bought my "facts" back then. The bogus 85 percent figure that CNN, Time and The New York Post breathlessly reported that year was incorrect. The number was 45 percent. Forty-Five percent is still high. This number also is a report card on universities and it means that 45% of their job placements did not succeed.

It does not take parents long to determine that the real proof of success, a proof not even asked for by the BBB, is the percentage of students that are employed in their major field. These statistics are even more dismal.

Yet, the colleges and universities continue to be in good standing? Something is wrong in America. An employed college graduate counts as employed even if they are tossing pizza dough at the Hut or tossing burgers on the grill at McDonalds, while waiting impatiently for the minimum wage to be raised to $15.00 per hour.

Let me repeat my thesis please. The vendor that provides the no value education—the college or university—is not held accountable for its failure to produce a functioning product. Of course, the finished products are graduates that more often than not nowadays are not at all capable of gaining the promises extended.

Parents must consider as the students are courted by the Admissions Department, and the Financial Aid Department, and all questions were answered in the positive—are they getting the truth?

Four or five years prior to graduation, these students and their parents are asked to sign letters of intent and even the more important quickie student loan applications to permit them to matriculate. Other papers in the pile included their loan applications, already filled out but for the signature. There is no guarantee form within the mass of paperwork, though the guarantee is even more than implied. The implied guarantee is worthless. Your child will be on the hook for the loan repayment.

Moreover, as if the student loan crisis has never happened, these same charlatans, dressed in their university plumage and finery are still permitted each and every year to continue to solicit and encourage a fresh batch of vulnerable 17 and 18-year olds to step into the financial abyss of a life that they will never be permitted to begin. And the institutions do so with vigor and complete impunity. Parents and student borrowers. must beware.

As a former college professor retired in 2011, I know that many parents and student graduates today are questioning the value of a university education. They have good reason to do so.

When the loan brokers have to wait until retirement years to collect the debt from social security or unemployment payments, can we all not admit that something is woefully wrong in America. Why would we encourage more of a bad thing? Where is our Congress?

The Obama Administration produced few really good jobs for fresh college graduates. Any jobs that were created were given to international student visa holders by the same universities that helped our children underachieve.

Should the colleges and universities not be able to take credit for job placements when the lucrative fields in which the graduate is placed includes areas of endeavor such as bartenders, waiters/waitresses, truck drivers, or other blue-collar type jobs?

Do the parents credit the University for these types of job placements—especially for graduate students? I think not.

From what I see from being on the front line, students in the bottom 25% of their class have about zero prospects for getting a first-job in their field. Those in the bottom 60% have a small chance. Most in these circumstances wish they could have that student loan decision, which they made at 17 or 18 years of age back again for a do-over.

Think about your own life/

What great decisions did you make when you were seventeen or eighteen? Now you know the extent of the problem. Student borrowers eventually learn that their huge loans, many over $100,000, may very well ruin their lives for years. For them, before they realize a modicum of success, they find their life has become a veritable debtors' prison, a dead end for someone the world is ready to call a *deadbeat,* despite the sheepskin hanging on the wall.

Where are the good jobs promised by the universities for all the money borrowed? At the same time that most graduates cannot find jobs, the jobs they do find pay less and less—even if it is in their chosen field. The average salary of college graduates has gone down 10% in the past ten years while inflation is growing at an ever-faster clip.

This is caused by a combination of a poor economy and because foreign graduates holding student visas take American jobs right after graduation. They work for substantially lower wages, especially if their visas are expired.

It helps to again offer the starkest statistic of all so all Americans understand this problem is not going away by itself. The percentages of college graduates living at home varies from survey to survey.

Forty-Five percent of college graduates from 2011 have had to swallow their pride and move home with mom and dad because they cannot afford life on their own. CNN had once reported the number at 85%. It doesn't take a rocket scientist to call out: "Houston, we have a problem!"

In 2005, Penelopetrunk.com wrote this about the problem:

> "In the list of what's hot and what's not, blowing all your money on an overpriced apartment is out and sleeping on the twin bed at your parents' house is in. Bobby Jackson is a senior at Williams College who will graduate this June. He will load up a moving container, head back to Washington, D.C. after graduation, and look for a public relations job from the comfort of his parents' home. Jackson typifies the remarkable shift of inter-generational attitudes when he declares, "I love hanging out with my parents."

> "According to market research company Twentysomething Inc., 65% of college seniors expect to live with their parents after graduation. The job web site MonsterTRAK reports that 50% of the class of 2003 continues to live at home. "Boomerangers" is what analysts call the twentysomethings moving back home, and the consensus among researchers (who grew up in an era when moving back was a sign of failure) is that being a boomeranger is a strategically sound way to head toward an independent life.

Chapter 10 The Impact of Foreign Students

Who has skin in the student debt game?

I must admit that I am surprised that nobody is calling out the universities for permitting more and more foreign students into their programs and then helping them gain employment ahead of American students. When foreign students graduate; guess whose jobs they take? According to their student visas, they are supposed to return to their country of origin. Once in America, however, they are not about to leave.

There are many groups that help students on their quest for employment in the US after graduating from an American university. Many students come to America to stay and, so they must be employed in order to remain legally in the country. Then again, the illegal residency option is often used when students cannot find jobs in their two-month opportunity period.

International Students taking American jobs is a big problem for American students trying to get a job. Ask the university placement office for the statistics on foreign student placements and for American student placements. Do not let them include the few students who go home in the denominator. Do not let them appear like it is not a problem for you.

Helping foreign students is a big industry

In their senior year, the very same universities and pillaging law firms line up to represent foreign students. They make recommendations for those who want to stay in America and not go home as required by the terms of their student visas—to which they agreed and swore. International students can take any of these four options:

- ✓ Enroll in the Optional Practical Training (OPT) and work in the United States for a year
- ✓ Get an H-1B (high tech work visa) to work at an American organization
- ✓ Attend graduate school in the US while working on gaining employment
- ✓ Simply do not go home and work underground
- ✓ Whereas we most often refer to these as foreign students; the universities like refer to them as International Students. Watch that trick designed to get American students to think less of themselves because they are not "international."!

How can a foreigner get a job in America after graduation as an International Student? There are a number of answers. Starting from the beginning, a student living in the US with an F-1 or J-1 (student) visa has 60 days to either enroll in another college or university for graduate studies or they can enroll in the OPT program to gain employment.

The *OPT* program is a very good deal for foreign students but not such a good deal for American students. It permits the J-1 and F-1 student visa status to be extended for one year so that the International student can gain professional training in their area of direct study. The application can take three to four months, so most students are advised early in their senior year to begin the process so that at graduation time, they may continue to stay in the country with employment. Their employment, by the way, may very well be the same job for which your son or daughter was aspiring. But, nobody is counting the Americans who are hurt by such programs.

So, after completing all course requirements for the degree, foreign students can gain full-time employment with American companies for one year. During that year, they can work to gain an H-1B visa for the following six years. This gives up to six additional years and then they can look to extend the H-1B again or work with their company sponsor to help them gain a green card, which is non-citizen, permanent residency in the US. Meanwhile our children who demand a living wage, are waiting for the USCIS to send these job poachers home. But, they never do!

Between 2009 and 2010, as less and less Americans students were being hired, the number of **OPT** students employed in American jobs rose by 14.43 percent.

Overall, if foreign students opt to stay in the US for a longer period of time, they simply get a company to sponsor them for the H-1B non-immigrant visa. This allows them to remain employed at that company for three years, and then they can get that extended for up to six or more years.

So, as the problem for young American student graduates gaining employment comes into focus, we see that a major destination for foreign students is the American workplace by achieving H-1B visas (college graduate – supposedly hi-techs).

International students from US university campuses are prime candidates for these positions. So, an innocent college education for a foreign student winds up being a job killer for American students. Yes, they do work for less. I know!

It is our Congress that permits this to occur by passing laws that are unfair to American citizens. And so, we find foreign graduates with degrees from the same universities as our children applying for jobs at the same companies that would hire our children if they were willing to work under the same conditions and for the same reduced wages as the foreign students.

Once an employer is found, the H-1B visa is granted and the foreign graduate takes the job for typically six years. Meanwhile American students go home to Mom and Dad simply to survive.

In other words, F-1, and J-1 visa holders are supposed to go home but they find university counselors or university lawyers to help get the deck stacked in their favor. They either use the OPT program or they go right to the H-1B visa program, so they do not have to go home.

Because they do not go home, your children cannot get jobs. Any questions?

The reason corporations hire foreigners over Americans is not because they are superior students but that they are a ready source of cheaper, yet still highly competent labor. Universities not only sell their foreign national graduates to corporations; they also hire more than their fair share of professors from the foreign national community. That is how I lost my own job; so, I know.

Many of those hired in universities have just received graduate degrees from American universities. In other words, for financial and diversity reasons, the universities prefer not to hire Americans for the faculty jobs, which they have available. Students are taught American subjects such as American History, by foreigners who can hardly speak the American language – English!

Congress permits colleges and universities to hire an unlimited number of foreigners as faculty or staff with the H-1B visa program. It is the exception to the nominal 65,000 visas permitted each year. American colleges and universities have a vested interest in foreign students and foreign workers. Ironically, they have no such interest in Americans, who pay their salaries.

I have witnessed universities firing existing faculty to replace them with younger foreign national professors willing to work for less money. Smaller universities will even outsource the legal part of the visa work to assure the foreign applicant a six-year H-1B visa. They will contract with immigration law firms and pay up to $10,000 or more per faculty member depending on the complexity of the case for the purpose of hiring a new faculty member who will work cheap for the sake of the university. How does this help American students?

Do you think that a "cheap" faculty has any effect on the quality of education our children receive? Does it have anything to do with the difficulty our children have in getting jobs?

It is really tough for Americans to get hired in US Universities since our Congress has seen fit to permit an unlimited number of foreign nationals to be hired as professors or staff at universities of all sizes in the US.

With more and more debt-saturated former students not being able to survive without their parents, this also has an impact on the indebted jobless-student borrower's ability to ever consider purchasing a home.

I know that I said this already, but it is how it is, and it is worth repeating. When American college graduates begin to be hired, the housing market will begin to boom again as will the Wedding Chapel business.

This major effect on the housing market and it will continue for years to come until the problem with student debt is solved. Who will buy the new homes if not the young? How can a college graduate that owes the equivalent of a huge house in student loan debt, ever be considered for purchasing a home? One problem will continue to feed the other until the student debt crisis is solved. Then, homes will again be sold in America at the proper sale amount.

No solution is simple. With 30% or more former students ultimately defaulting on their loans, and many more trapped in a financial abyss, from which they may never escape, Congress can certainly create a better way to help the borrower, the housing market, and the taxpayer, all at the same time. It might not benefit foreigners or the universities, but it would help parents and the students that got sucked into promises from university pitchmen that were as powerful as the best infomercials you have ever seen on TV.

Chapter 11 A Few Other Solid Solutions

Reduce student borrower's interest rates

We have already discussed a number of solutions. Congress and the President must act now. Short of debtor's prison, I would suggest that Congress assure that in times when no person in the US can find a savings account earning more than a percent (or two) interest rate; that the lenders should not be able to inflict usury rates on students.

This is common practice today and it leads many student borrowers to default. Why should students pay 6% to 10% while they can earn only 1%? Unless the government is trying to hurt former students, it makes no sense.

Student borrowers need to have their interest rates capped at something that is affordable. What good does it do if 30% default today and perhaps 50% will default ten years from now? How does this help anybody but the guardians of the mythical debtor's prison?

I would like Congress to help me understand why the Stafford Loan interest percentage was raised to almost 7% when only a rare bank pays more than one percent interest. When today's borrowers can get a mortgage for just over 3%, and the best savings rate that the most lucrative banks give is less than 1.5%, why would our government ever permit the Stafford loan or any loan for that matter to be so much higher than the savings interest rate.

On the Sallie Mae Web Site, they advertise an APR of 9.72% for new student loans. This is ridiculous unless you run a government funded debtor's prison, or your background is the loan shark business.

Nobody wants defaults on these loans or any other loans, but the terms have become so usurious and oppressive that the law of unintended consequences is beginning to deal many defaults right from the top of the deck. This must be solved post haste.

Why not permit defaulters a new shot at paying back their loans? Put a package together that includes taking students out of default status temporarily no more interest for two or three years. Let everything counts towards the principle. It sure is better getting something than nothing and the defaulter may come back and begin to pay again.

Bring back the bankruptcy option

All debt should be treated equally. A drug dealer can declare bankruptcy on credit card bills, but a student cannot get a break in massive debt situation with usurious interest rates. How is that?

As we are all aware, Congress has taken the bankruptcy option off the table for students so for many, there is no way out of the hole. There is not even a speck of light at the end of the tunnel. Is this really what we want or should Congress fashion a solution that brings back some hope to what is now a situation that makes many of our young citizens either hopeless or feeling hopeless. Tell me the difference?

After assuring very low, reasonable, payback interest rates, just a hair above the Treasury note, I would recommend Congress make the student loan game fair again by rounding in the student borrower's favor rather than the lender. Simply trace back the last few iterations of legislation and instead of making students targets of corrupt lenders, strip those lenders of the powers that the Congress has given them.

Let me offer some examples:

Most of the laws enacted by Congress have hurt those who do not have the means to pay back their student loans at the rate demanded by Sallie Mae or other legitimate "loan sharks" in the student loan industry.

For example, Congress enacted the 2005 Bankruptcy Abuse Prevention and Consumer Protection Act, which presupposes that students; who are in fact bankrupt, can be enslaved in a debtor's prison and through prayer, and perhaps some great prison poker skills, can somehow come up with the money to pay off their student loans.

This gift from Congress had a number of sweet surprises for students, who at the time were looked upon as the bad guys! By the way, Congress still treats our kids as the bad guys.

The big surprise in this law is that Student loans that were not guaranteed by the federal government were henceforth deemed to not be eligible to be discharged in bankruptcy. This became law on October 17, 2005. In other words, when credit card companies find out that you used your credit card to pay for a course, they can come after you under this law. If you bought beer instead of education, they could not touch you.

Would any American think that the laws for credit card debt would be less severe than the laws for students trying to gain an American education? What limitations are there on credit card purchases? They can be used for anything. Student loans can be used only for education, so why would Congress treat credit card debt in a more favorable light than student debt? One word—lobbyists!

Additionally, to show its utter disdain for students who cannot get jobs and are forced to default, Congress changed the Higher Education Act and eliminated all statutes of limitations for the collection of student loan debt – even those from the past.

If I don't say so again, all of the provisions of this act should be repealed to give students a fair shot, rather than promote an even higher default rate.

With this law, out of nowhere, students who once had a tough time paying off their loans in times of leniency on student debt, which had passed the time specified in the statute of limitations, and who were thus free from their debt in the 70's and 80's, again found themselves getting billed for the forgiven debt. The government was only kidding.

These guys are now in their 50's 60's and 70's, and social security is being garnished.

Again, their arrearage plus their remaining debt amount became a collectible debt! This gave the loan sharks and collection agencies a new source of revenue. But for the unfortunate students or the grandmas who secured the debt, they became outlaws as their debt remained uncollectible but due nonetheless.

And we know how nice the collectors are when they call at 7 or 8 in the AM.

Here is another goodie. The law now permits lenders to lie about student loans and it is OK! Yes, student loans are specifically exempted from coverage under the Truth in Lending Act (TILA). They are also now specifically exempted from state usury laws…lending money at an unreasonably high interest rate. Charge what you want to students but nobody else.

If the student loan sharking agencies raise the rate to 55%, you must pay the rate. Additionally, most student loan guarantors do not have to adhere to the 1988 Federal Trade Commission legislation requiring an adherence to Fair Debt Collection and Practices in pursuing defaulted borrowers. Thank you, Congress.

Why not? With over8 million students in default, and parents more and more involved in the game, how does this help anybody? Are the debt collectors included in the private industry job gains the prior administration liked to claim?

Please do not get the wrong idea. There were days in which students graduated and then laughed at the idea of paying back their student loans and eventually the loan went away. These are not those days, and these are not the debtors of which I speak. I am talking about our kids.

I am not looking for a return to those, days but the pendulum has gone too far the other way and Congress must fix it. People are getting hurt in many ways and I read just today of a young lady with stage 2 curable cancer who was being hounded so much by student loan debt collectors that she took her own life. I am sure there are more situations like this.

Is this what we really want for America? Should we punish our young adults when they are young, and then expect them to grow up to treat the world fairly?

Anybody who checks what the student lenders are doing, and how harshly they treat everybody—people who do not have two nickels to rub together—would admit that somehow a big sin has been perpetrated against the young adults in America and our Federal Government not only permits it; it encourages it! Shame on our Congress for allowing this.

Permitting seventeen and eighteen-year olds to sign up for a life in a debtor's prison is a sin just like the children, just over ten years old, working in the mines prompted the child labor laws.

So, let's solve the problem in a fair way that does not take the life out of the most alive people in America—our children. The recommended solution keeps income flowing to repay the loans and gets the loan sharking, unfair collection tactics, and garnishment of social security out of the student loan business. It is worth a hard look.

Stop new student borrowing abuse

The first step after helping students repay loans is to stop additional student loan borrowing abuse. It is not always best for students to go to college. Getting a position as a truck driver, five years after high school, with a college degree and a huge debt does not help anybody but the university. Getting that job five years earlier helps a part-time student immensely.

First of all, I recommend giving all the defaulted student borrowers a second chance at making it right. That brings eight million lost participants back into the game. If each give just one dollar a year, that is $5 million more dollars a year than would have arrived otherwise. Everything counts. Let's ask for a buck with options for more than one buck, but let's take the buck because at least we have made contact.

Graduated repayment schedule

Without a total forgiveness, which is the best idea, every student borrower with current income should have to pay something back on their loan but it cannot be the equivalent of being in a debtor's prison. I recommend a progressive payback schedule (like the progressive income tax) based on adjusted gross income.

For those borrowers approaching default, I would add a new type of forbearance in which no interest is charged for several years. Borrowers feel better when they reduce the principal with some of each payment. Once the student goes into default status, they may be inclined to stay there and never come back.

Up to the poverty line, let's set the percentage at 1% so everybody pays something against their debt. Set the minimum rate of payment in the schedule after the poverty line at 3%. Yes, everybody pays something. For somebody who has already defaulted, forgive the interest payments so the borrower has a chance to climb out of debt. I would suggest a bracket for each 5% after that up to a maximum rate of 25% of income for the highest bracket.

Let's look at a typical IRS schedule. The 2012 tax brackets will suffice to get an idea on how to structure this:

Tax Bracket Single
10% Bracket $0 – $8,700
15% Bracket $8,700 – $35,350
25% Bracket $35,350 – $85,650
28% Bracket $85,650 – $178,650
33% Bracket $178,650 – $388,350
35% Bracket over $388,350

Using the same type of structure, this is a first cut at an equitable minimum payment schedule. To get somebody restarted I would recommend a $1.00 per month for a few years to get them accustomed to paying something. Note that everybody who makes as little as $100.00 per year should pay 1% (something) per year on the second bracket, etc. up to the poverty level:

Student Loan Repayment on Yearly Adjusted Gross
$1.00 per month rather than a default
1% Bracket $100 – $11,170 (poverty line)
5% Bracket $11,170 – $40,000
10% Bracket $40,000 – $80,000
15% Bracket $80,000 – $120,000
20% Bracket $120,000 – $220,000
25% Bracket over $220,000

I am not suggesting this is the perfect chart, but it is the right idea. It may be too little or too much. It looks fair to me. We need to ask the people in these circumstances and set the rates, so undue burdens are not the rule. A key element is that interest stops for several years so that the student borrower accepts the loan principle as a debt and they can watch it decrease.

This is just a first look. Ultimately it all depends on a fair interest rate. If the rate or the process is not fair, it will not work. Therefore, Congress must change it as the graduated schedule must be fair and it must lead to the student borrower being free of debt at some point.

It is designed to eventually get the loans paid off but even if it does not, nobody should go broke paying off a debt that is due. So many young people look at say, their Sallie Mae payment, and they know they can't do it ever; so, they default and never look back.

For heaven's sake we do not want the cream of the crop young people in America in any form of debtor's prison. Because Congress permitted unscrupulous colleges and universities, loan sharks, and corrupt loan collectors to saddle seventeen and eighteen-year olds with bad loans and life-changing-debt, we owe our young a reprieve. We owe them a better deal. I know a man with a philosophy of "Make America Great Again," would feel the same.

Of course, even with the repayment schedules above, in no instance should anybody have to pay more than the minimum monthly payment in their official payback schedule for their loan even if they could afford it. Government should donate all student loan profits to help the students who need it the most get out of default.

When somebody becomes a "deadbeat' in the student loan system; they have few other options than to hide from the collector. Those who paid off their loans do not know the scourge of such harassment.

Parents often must change their phone numbers and get unlisted numbers and ask their neighbors to not acknowledge them, so they can protect their children from the incessant phone calls. In America, there must be a better way. Nobody asks illegal aliens on welfare to pay anything back. Why is that? It is not fair.

To help pay for the reprieve, if Congress chooses not to reach into US Assets as pointed out in earlier chapters, I would also set up a means for any taxpayer to donate a $1.00 and greater by checking a box on their tax refund and having it directed towards the paying down of all student loans.

I would also recommend a web site in which anybody can donate by credit card to help pay down the cumulative student loan debt for American kids trying to better themselves. Payments would be apportioned only to those whose debts are in default, in such a way as to not encourage defaulting.

I do not believe in the free lunch. So, any program must involve the debtor, though it is very unfair to expect 17 or 18-year old's to be able to pay back a huge mortgage. The program also should involve the co-signors, who never would have expected the universities to make it more difficult for their graduates to get real jobs by helping foreigners ahead of Americans.

The student debtor and the co-signor were both duped by the academic institutions to keep the student at the institution for four or five or even six years for an undergraduate degree, though the institution was working against the parents promoting foreign students to employers rather than Americans.

We all know that universities make a big promise about the value and the future promise of an education for a successful graduate. Yet, they have taken no responsibility when the graduate is never employed.

Before any reduced opportunity for retirement (garnishment of social security etc.) should be inflicted against the loan cosigners, the cash collectors should come after the universities for promises un-kept. My final recommendation set therefore as in Chapter 1 and 2 is a bit more controversial.

All of this money that former students have signed for or have paid and will pay over the years has already has found its way into the coffers of universities across the nation. Despite being the only party to whom the proceeds have been given, the universities seemingly have no skin in the loan game.

And, since the product of the universities, the students, our children have not been able to achieve the American Dream as promised by the Admissions Counselors, and the Financial Aid Counsellors, there should be recourse.

Since such universities encourage foreign students to take jobs in the US upon graduation and they also hire foreign faculty even when Americans are available, universities are a part of the problem. The recourse should be even more obvious.

In this regard, as noted in Chapter 1, I would ask the Congress to enact legislation to make colleges and universities a part of the financial solution, providing the following:

1. Individual students, who failed to meet reasonable expectations regarding the promised value of their degrees should be able to sue colleges and universities for a part of their student debt balance.

2. Government should collect a fee of 5% of the university's gross revenue up to 25% (similar notion to the student payback schedule with different values for gross revenue) – at least something. This is to be applied to paying down all student loans for graduates or attendees of that particular college or university. The minimum payment would

be a factor of the student default rate for the institution and the percentage of gross revenue. The exact formula will need some work.

3. Severely limit the number of foreign students admitted until the US unemployment rate is 2.5% and cap the number permitted to obtain work visas after graduation to a smaller / reasonable number. Work with American students first for jobs and assistance. No foreign student gets help until all Americans get help.

4. Limit the number of H-1B visas for faculty to a very small number perhaps 2% of total faculty. Today the number is unlimited and often American students in American universities are shortchanged because their teachers are not fluent in English.

5. Assure the H-1B faculty member on worker visa returns to the home country after the visa expires with no renewals. Employee visa holders should not be permitted to get in line for green card or citizenship if they have already been granted faculty status. This is unfair to American professors.

6. Reduce all non-University H-1B visas from 85,000 (65,000) to 2,000 until the unemployment rate goes to 2%.

These recommendations would not necessarily affect those students who are doing very well and can afford to pay off their debt through the normal payment schedules. However, in as much as the Congress is encouraged to remove the ability for financial companies to loan shark any student loan debtor, this plan is designed to help us all.

Even the tax payers will be helped as the five million plus, who today have no hope will be able to begin paying at least a small percentage on their loan. Eventually they will be able to pay a higher percentage, and then hopefully, they will also be able to buy a house and begin a family. The greatest advantage of all in this program is nobody will feel they are in a debtor's prison with no escape.

Chapter 12 Preventing New Massive Student Debt

Solve Both Big Issues!

There are two big issues with the student debt crisis as follows:

1. How to prevent students from accumulating huge student loan debts in the future.
2. How to deal with the $1.45 trillion student debt already accumulated.

This chapter deals with item # 1. Other chapters in this book have addressed #2. There are a number of clever approaches being discussed in academic and government circles regarding both of these issues.

My university wrote me a letter

On the student side, Indiana State University is ahead of the curve with the most sensible notion yet on new student debt. It is documented that 53% of students who are attending college have no idea that they are accumulating a massive loan debt. I know it is hard to believe. They have no idea that when the student graduates or drops out of college, they will be asked to pay the loan down immediately.

In the flurry of getting admitted to a favorite university, how the bill gets paid is most often the last thing discussed with the admissions counsellor if discussed at all. College loan sharks exist in private industry, but admissions counsellors are often just as guilty in convincing poor students to attend college by taking a huge, easy to-get loan.

Mom and dad and junior and missy are lulled by the hype of the notion of attending college at their choice of universities. They fill out all their forms as everybody else and the admissions department and financial aid department make a determination how much they can afford out of pocket and how much has to come in the form of various grants and aid packages including loans of various kinds.

Nobody considers whether they can pay it back as the assumption is that graduation will bring with it automatically, a high-paying job

Getting a college loan is easier than getting a car loan. It is easier than getting a pack of cigarettes as a five-year-old. That is why many students add the car cost onto the student loan package and they take out a little extra for smokes. Nobody convinces them that there is a down-side to all that debt. In fact, until they meet the piper four to six years later, it all feels pretty good spending money.

The university tuition is always set high especially today with so many sources of funding for students. Giving a little aid to a student is no big deal today. It helps to remember the result of such a system places 70% of students who graduate in a debtor position with tens of thousands of dollars of student loans due.

When the package comes to the student along with an acceptance letter, there is euphoria on the part of the parents and the student. Johnnie and Janie are able to attend a great college and whatever the loan amount is as part of the package is simply another part of the yes vote when the student signs for the package with mom and dad's permission.

The next semester after the summer hiatus, the student begins to matriculate. There appears to be no downside until the debt is due.

Indiana has decided to be a lot more honest with its students and its new student loans are down by almost 20% while the number of students accepting admission is about the same. How is it that Indiana's students do not need as much funding as those students in other universities?

It's simple. Indiana tells them they are going into debt and to think carefully about the amount of debt they are about to take on as the debt from the loan will have to be paid back and it will affect their lives after graduation.

Those looking at the Indiana program and finding that it makes a lot of common-sense are suggesting the notion be more widespread than just one university in the nation. Based on Indiana's success, more schools are getting on the band-wagon.

It should be illegal to grant a loan until a prospective student attends a mini course on the effects of college debt upon life after graduation, and they pass a financial impact understanding test.

Many are suggesting that informative truthful letters should be sent from high schools to moms and dads and the high school students well before the prospective college student chooses whether to go to college or focus on vocational training. It's like telling the whole story and not giving universities and loan sharks the edge.

The crowds of new vigilantes against massive student debt also suggest that each college administer a quiz to incoming freshmen, to make sure they understand the kind of debt they are about to assume. A mandatory SAT-like exam should be put together that provides a risk profile for each student that should be used to assess whether the student qualifies to be granted a loan.

The tests in many ways would help to insulate colleges against nuisance lawsuits later, when students can't find jobs and they blame their college administrators for not disclosing the full extent of their debt. But, more than vindicating the institutions of higher learning, the idea is to provide an honest wakeup call that hits the student and parents between the eyes.

It must tell them that success is not a sure thing but the debt that will be accumulated is a sure thing. Quite frankly such a message may even prompt the borrower to become a much better student.

Intuitive solution not on the US table

Why is it that if you and I now know and those in charge know that the system of today is built to disadvantage our young, why is it permitted? Americans should have been informed years ago that the system is rigged to punish kids for trying to succeed. All of the privileges granted to loan sharks, and collection sharpies including the right to lie, and the permission to increase interest at any time, needs to be understood. Actually, Congress should get rid of these privileges, don't you think?

Millennials, the kids who are most affected by the student loan rigged system, even after graduation simply do not get it. They would be prepared to vote for the same people who created their dilemma even if it creates pain for other young people.

Donald Trump is a one of a kind human being. He hates rigged systems. He got his wealth from a financial bump from dad when young and then he had to work hard to become extremely successful. He loves being extremely successful and wants everybody else to take a fair shot at success.

Today's normal student debt system creates kids whose options have become a life from 23 to 65 years of age in a debtor's prison. Of course, the miserable life is preceded by a great four or five-year stint of raucous parties and an enjoyable life on campus, mixed with a little studying.

College students often get to live at a great college and perhaps gain a degree in their field of choice. In today's world depending on circumstances such as their grades, may not be good enough for a job. While on campus, however, life is swell. But, when the first bill comes, the fun stops.

Sometimes it is more prudent for middle of the road students to say "no," for a few years before going to school. Try life in the workforce before going back for a degree. It would avoid a lot of heartache trying to pay back $100,000 or more in student debt with a $15,000 a year job while living with mom and dad.

Colleges and universities and even parents package the deal so sweetly that the new high school seniors cannot say no. After the four or five-year great time post high school, and no job, their life is over for a long time. They are placed into the bucket with all of the other 70%, who are responsible for the $1.45 trillion of student loan borrowing in America.

Sorry, there is no escape once a high school student elects to take the plunge into the student debt pool. Congress saw to that. Congress decided that there is no way out of student debt and there is no way to make the pain any less severe than having the young adults in America believe their lives are being spent in a debtor's prison with no escape.

Meanwhile the same Congress has tricks so that those related to them in their work effort can escape without owing anything. No Virginia, life is not fair unless you are a Congressman.

So, is there an intuitive solution to high school students unknowingly signing up for a life of bondage devised intentionally so that a prestigious university can collect cold hard cash from unknowing student debtors and deliver little in exchange? A job! Sorry! Universities get jobs for foreign nationals not privileged Americans.

Yes, there is an intuitive solution but millennials I fear would not get it. I can recall that when I went to college and worked with the janitorial staff to get part of my tuition paid, the head janitor had a sign outside his office. It read "A college education is a four-year loaf on dad's bread, and the product comes out fresh with a lot of crust." I never forgot that.

I understood the truth. I did not have the risk today's babes in the woods have in dealing with college loan sharks. I was working my way through with just a few very affordable loans and an academic scholarship.

Yet, I understood as these gentleman on the janitorial staff knew that there were a lot of bold and brazen contemporaries of mine who were convinced that they knew everything. They felt that any help given to them was well deserved. I had met them. I originally believed that they were smarter than I until the first tests started coming back and then I knew they were made of wind.

I have three millennial children and like Donald Trump's brood, my kids appreciate everything they get. I thank God for that. They tell me that their peers respect little about the old America and do not care about America as their parents do. They have not experienced America as I know it, or my children know it.

I regret that for them. Our country is such a wonderful place compared to all others. I wish millennials were not forced to listen to the labored breathing of coffee-breathed liberal progressive professors in ultra-Marxist universities. They are inundated with anti-Americanism all day long by people who do not care if they get a job or if they can ever pay off their college loans.

As a professor myself, I know these people and I understand why our young in America are so distraught about America. Yet, there is no rational explanation other than the fraud perpetrated on all Americans by the elite academicians whose disdain for rugged individualism or the freedom to be an individual has affected the gentlest minds in America—our young adults. Millennials!

Many young parents say that the first time they realized how smart their parents were, was when they had their own children.

Unfortunately, the current world brought to us by Democrats, who love the idea of a dependent American, are happy with a world full of student debt with no escape. They are OK with foreigners, legal or not, holding all the respectable jobs in America. Our smartest college graduates are sunk in massive debt.

Millennials have been convinced by their coffee-breath professors that the reason they can never enjoy a family, a home, a fine job, and hope for the future is because America sucks. This is not true. As a professor and as a guy who knows these liars, I am so sorry that the students in their charge, millennials as we call them, have fallen for this claptrap.

The fact is that America is the best place to be unless you want somebody else to control your life.

So, what is the solution? We must rely on our "honest" government to get the right message out as early as possible about the risks of huge debt and the potential of no prospects for a good life. When our government is dishonest, we must replace it at the top with people like Donald Trump, and at the bottom with people who are smart like us, who love America.

Not every teacher and not every government employee and not every politician is against the people, but it sure seems too many are. They are guided by a corrupt press which forces all Americans to fight hard to gain the truth. We must demand that our children learn that a college education may very well cost a student a better life if it is not planned and accepted properly. The sooner the better.

College must no longer be the default for all high school students and all the other choices need to be explored by students as they once had been. Kuder tests and other vocational tests need to be brought back and implemented. White-collar professionals should help form white collar potential career paths and blue-collar professionals should present the same for the trades and the physical work place.

In terms of making sure we do not add more bad debt to the $1.45 Trillion currently owed, we need to make sure that each of those who might accept debt for a larger opportunity, do so with their eyes wide open and with the facts all known.

I have two last suggestions for the period in which all the college signings are done by the high school student.

1. Online course
2. Preprinted complete information forms

1. Each student who plans to attend college should be required to complete an online course of study in his or her junior or senior year, and perhaps in both years, in which they learn about all the specifics about the opportunities of a college degree. The material should include the risks of debt and other methods of paying for tuition, room, board, & books.

2. In addition to the letters and the courses and the brochures that explain to high school students the potential for devastating lifelong debt, the state and national governments should add a student debt information form that is as formal as all the other federal and state and lender / borrower forms.

It should be prefilled based on the student database, with specific information about the borrower. Based on the borrower's high school record and the track record of success for the chosen institution, a computer model should produce a probability of success, calculated based on past histories.

Additionally, all the anticipated costs and the anticipated payback period and amounts should be preprinted along with anything else that would be helpful to the student making an informed decision about debt. This should be regardless of its impact on the university of choice.

Income Share Agreement

There is another notion becoming popular out there to use to finance college instead of borrowing to the gills. It is called an Income Share Agreement. In this, students promise a portion of their future earnings and the burden is not as severe in most cases compared to student loans. These agreements are emerging on the scene with rapidity, so I present them as an alternative. You may study them at the following URL:

http://www.businessinsider.com/income-share-agreements-help-students-pay-for-college-loan-alternative-2017-3

Chapter 13 Reminder: Cost of an Undergraduate Degree

The plight of the poor rich

Let's talk about what a major cost a college education has become. It is so huge that it cannot be taken trivially as it can help float or it can totally sink your life.

The first of my unnumbered thoughts is that rich people own the world. There is no question about it. No argument will change that fact. Theoretically, if they wanted to, they could simply eliminate the rest of us. That surely would not be fair, but they could do it as they own all the major resources, the armies, and the armaments.

We could probably throw in for good measure that they own the leadership in most if not all countries. More than likely, the only things that keep them from taking over everything is #1, they do not trust the other rich guys, and #2, there would be no services they could buy if we were not available, walking the earth, to perform the services for them.

I am not rich; but I think I have made it to someplace into the middle class. I have a BS and an MBA. Great rich people, through taxes and through contributions to my college and to the government made it possible for me to win a half scholarship for achievement and a half-tuition loan (National Defense Student Loan) because my parents did not have enough money to send me to college. Two halves do make a complete whole in my case, but in the end, I was responsible for just $50.00 a year from my private funds.

I was seventeen years old as a freshman until the beginning of my second semester in college. Like today's college students, I was simply tickled to pieces to be able to go to a great college. I also got a job at the school for $1.25 per hour under the Federal Work Study Program.

This was the minimum wage at the time. This again was mostly paid for by some rich person's taxes. The college paid 10% for my work, and the federal government paid 90% of my hourly rate.

I am very happy that rich people exist, and I am glad they share their gains with regular people. I was a clear beneficiary. I do agree that the pendulum has gone too far today with a tyranny of the underclass against the rich.

Today the rich still pay most of the taxes and they sponsor an awful lot of good stuff for regular people. I am glad they exist. I am not at all jealous. I do believe it would be a good thing, not a bad thing to become rich through hard work or even by winning the lottery. Good fortune helps us all be better people. I thank God that rich people treated me so well growing up. It sure made a difference in my life.

Today, the school I attended, whose tuition way back in time was $950 per year with no special fees other than graduation, is now $34,720 per year. That figure includes fees for all kinds of activities. Those amenities all cost money.
The full load without books estimated at $1500 per year is in the table on the following page:

COSTS	RESIDENT	COMMUTER
Tuition and Fees (full-time)	$34,720	$34,720
Average Room and Board	$12,136	N/A
Total	$46,856	$34,720

That's well over $100,000 if you are lucky to finish in four years. A little-known statistic is that only 1% of the students pay the full amount. In other words, 99% receive some type of package which includes grants (not paid back) and loans (must be paid back).

It is all bundled nicely so that the student merely has to say OK with his or her John Hancock to be off to college the following fall. There is no documentation that I found that discusses risks.

AWARDS	RESIDENT	COMMUTER
Average Financial Aid Package	$23,472	$24,911
Average Gift (Scholarship, Grant) Aid	$17,730	$17,914

Some people see the combination of the Admissions Departments and the Financial Aid Departments of universities and colleges in much the same way as a business views its marketing department and its accounting department.

Though Admissions or Enrollment Management (a more exact term) sounds better than marketing, marketing is its job nonetheless. Its mission is to convince the best students to come to the university at the listed price with some discounts.

Let's suppose the name of this college is Student Loan University (SLU). Here are some of the words a typical high school student would find when dealing with the shrewd marketers at SLU to entice the prospective student to go along with the "AID" package, which they receive:

When determining the cost of a college education, one should also take into consideration the value. U.S. News & World Report has ranked SLU among America's best colleges for 18 straight years and Barrons consistently considers us one of the best buys in college education. [Notice there is no guarantee that you will do well.]

Approximately 99% of all full-time students attending SLU receive financial assistance, with the average scholarship being $10,815 [that leaves 34,720-$10815 =$23,905 per year for you to pay]. We encourage every student to apply for financial aid no matter what their family circumstances are. Only after you have applied and been considered for all available assistance will you have a true idea of what your costs will be.

SLU offers a payment plan through Tuition Management Systems (TMS), which allows families to make monthly payments on the balance of tuition, fees, room and board less any financial aid received.

If the cost of the Tuition Management System seems too high for a family, it helps for students to remember that after four years of accumulated interest, the same plan for the next four years would be even more expensive. Sometimes, college tuition at the institution of choice is simply too expensive and a nice community college and / or state college combination may deliver the same benefits at substantially lower costs.

Chapter 14 For-Profit Schools

Should for profit schools even exist?

For-Profit institutions have probably funded a few scientists who created solutions for problems that are making life better across the world. Their stories are not told because, so many have failed in life because they were artificially lifted to be among the gifted and they had few gifts at all from God that a college education would amplify.

So, another increasingly popular topic in the student debt debate is for-profit colleges, which have come under increased scrutiny in recent years. As an explanation, for-profit colleges are often exactly what they sound like – colleges run by substantial, publicly traded companies, or private equity firms, who answer to the interests of shareholders, and their key interest is to make a profit.

In search of returns, they do not necessarily provide the best shakes for the best students. These institutions recruit high numbers of students with questionable methods, and they do not always deliver on their promises. The institutional concerns towards students at these schools tend to begin and end with tuition payment, regardless of who pays the bill.

For-profit schools have made a substantial impact on federal student loan debt on the negative side of the ledger. At for-profits, for example, 96 percent of students take out loans, and the average student ends up with $40,000 in debt. Remember there are 50% in many cases if this were a mean, who have substantially higher debt.

In addition, a 2012 study found that as the government raised federal aid amounts, for-profits closely matched these increases with surges in tuition. They knew they could get away with it as the loans were there to cover tuition. Next, one can argue parallels between for-profit student loans, and subprime mortgage loans during the crisis. Neither were based on the best financial thinking available and there was a lot of greed involved.

In the Great Recession, the underwriters of subprime mortgages did not pay much attention to the creditworthiness of the loans, just as for-profits in the Student Loan Industry (SLI) do not care for the creditworthiness of students when advising towards federal direct programs. Students pay big prices for being sucked in by such charlatans. The charlatans always get paid and the students always are riddled with debt that must be paid back.

All in all, during the mortgage crisis, the government at least ruled that mortgages could not exceed the value of the home. Maybe the value of a for-profit education should have been taken into consideration during the boom of these institutions (unfortunately, calculating the value would be easier said than done).

On the bright side, increased oversight and regulation has improved the for-profit education sector in recent years. Today, the government has begun "requiring them to prove that, on average, students' loan payments amount to less than eight per cent of their annual income. Schools that fail this test four years in a row have their access to federal loans cut off, which would effectively put them out of business. So, there is a role for a lobbyist everywhere we turn.

In the past few years, the number of borrowers has decreased, and for-profit default rates have somewhat improved. The trade-off in regulation, however beneficial to the debt program overall, does have important effects on the traditional for-profit attendee. Many students at for-profits are older, part-time individuals returning to school to earn a degree.

These individuals returning to school to better themselves are obviously a huge part of the target audience of the federal loan program. Thus, if the government is going to tighten the reigns on for-profits, something must give to help these students in other respects (such as through increased funding towards community colleges or public institutions).

Potential Solutions

Now that a vast overview of the student debt market has been documented, the most significant part of this debate must be examined – solutions. By far the most frustrating part of the American political landscape today remains the constant finger pointing and grumbling without delivering viable solutions.

In all the research conducted, dozens of reporters, politicians, and journalists have proposed protests on education and student debt, but no reform. Reform is what we need but what type of reform we get depends on some honesty in government. Can we trust anybody? I trust Donald J. Trump.

You may know that at least one presidential candidate went as far as to say that when it comes to education on an international level, "We're twenty-sixth in the world. Twenty-five countries are better than us at education. And some of them are like third world countries. With Congress's rules for loan sharks, the US is morphing into a third-world country."

For the record, this cannot be even remotely verified by any valid news or research source. This candidate also offered other such groundbreaking insights on the Department of Education: "You could cut that way, way, way down". This is certainly a scintillating opinion, and as much as I would encourage all American citizen to be well informed on such complex and important issues, I would not dismiss any great ideas simply because somebody in the mainstream media suggests that I do so.

Legislative/Political Suggestions

A number of legislators, politicians, and presidential candidates have made a wide variety of suggestions. Donald Trump of course solves both the problem of $1.45 trillion of debt as well as how to prevent its creeping increase.

While there are hundreds of ideas and potential fixes to the student debt problem, I would like to specifically discuss the ones that appear most valid, without attributing them to anybody.

I've already discussed Trump ideas and they are good. The other ideas and proposals are also from Donald Trump, as well as Jeb Bush, Marco Rubio, Lamar Alexander, and Mitch Daniels.

To begin, there are some proposals to simplify and improve the student loan crisis. One proposes that limits be set on the federal direct loan program – allowing for a $50,000 line of credit that can be drawn upon or paid back throughout one's educational pursuit.

There are few specifics on this, but it clearly would reduce debt and it would force students into getting the best bang for the buck. It would also prevent regular Joe's from soiling the linens at Harvard and Princeton.

There is also a proposal that for each increment of $10,000 borrowed, students would pay back 1% of their income for 25 years. Some initiatives for improvement here involve more real-world experience through internships, certifications, etc., and also through a database listing of various statistics on schools to educate individuals on their decision (unemployment rates, earnings, graduation rates, and others)

Others echo this plan in some ways, saying that there should be movements in accreditation reform and income-based repayment.

Marco Rubio knows the pains of student debt. After paying off his nearly $150,000 in student loans, he contends that, "People should be allowed, through internships and work study and online courses and classroom courses and life and work experience, to be able to package all of that together into the equivalent of a degree." My problem with that is who is it that grants the degree, Joe Biden?

Some Senators have advocated for making the student loan system much simpler. Through simplification of the FAFSA form that each individual must fill out for student aid, many more individuals will not be deterred by the current 108-question complex document.

Mitch Daniels is always deferred to now that he has ascended to the throne at Purdue. Daniels argues for the use of a more privatized system of income-share agreements, an idea championed by Nobel Prize winning economist Milton Friedman in the 1950's.

Under an income-share agreement, or ISA, students would pay for their education through a fixed percentage of their income after graduation for an allotted period of time. Typical rates are anywhere from 3 to 15 percent of income, and 5 to 20 years.

Daniels launched his pilot junior and senior class program in the fall semester 2016. With Purdue having a reputation as a STEM major (science technology engineering and math) hub, many of its students would benefit from favorable rates and low percentages of income requested. Sociology majors beware.

Industry Experts

The preponderance of expert opinion says that the increasing student debt load is simply unsustainable, and policy changes must be made to help both the federal budget and the students. Next, they suggest that this change comes more from the private sector and less from the government side. Having multiple entities to share the risk of the loans – having "skin in the game" – would surely increase the quality of the loans made and the probability of their subsequent repayment.

Increased help from colleges would also be beneficial; most importantly, schools have begun to advertise better their debt and graduation statistics to let students know what to expect. Lastly, the importance of finding out how to help those that are already ensnared by loads of debt is being pushed forward.

For those who have taken out large amounts and are stuck with no form of repayment, there must be more help in place to get these Americans back on their feet. Other than default, there are few options other than skipping the country.

The great thing about ISA's, if implemented properly, would be that if all does not work out for a student, they would not be deep in a hole of debt from which escape was not possible. Overall, there will hopefully be major changes in the future to save the student debt amount from growing larger, and from convincing students who do not belong in college to stay out or be prepared to pay the price.

From delving into the world of student debt, I know that the problem can be solved if America wants to solve it. Some have developed very complex models with many assumptions. The debt and ISA model can be adjusted based on different median incomes, costs of capital for both debt and ISA, portion of income shared, interest on the debt, etc.

Experts in the business have proposed that the United States make ISAs a more functional funding vehicle. They note that there is currently bipartisan legislation awaiting approval laying the groundwork for ISAs. They offer that the law lays out limits on time of repayment, portion of income, and states that ISAs would not be dischargeable in bankruptcy, like student debt currently.

It also follows what many early adopters have already been using, by limiting repayments only to years where an individual makes $18,000 or more. Once a groundwork like this has been created, ISAs will be much easier to write up from a legal standpoint, and from a high school student perspective, they will be easier to swallow.

Though I don't like the idea of businesses making a profit on students, I keep looking at some of the features of ISA's which are beginning to make them look more attractive. If investors make a killing, government must step in and limit the student's loss.

One would argue that the government should develop a "one size fits all" type of ISA agreement or debt/equity blend, and private companies develop their own more competitive ISAs or blends. Through the private versions, students would be able to receive more favorable rates based on thorough credit analysis looking at the individual's history, proposed university, major, and other significant factors.

This would encourage individuals to choose better, more affordable schools, and in turn encourage schools to improve their graduation and debt rates. In addition, through this system, losses can be diversified away due to the law of large numbers. With a pool of students large enough, losses from those that are not as successful can be made up for by the higher performing individuals.

Most importantly though, students who are less successful would no longer be burdened until death with large amounts of debt, which in some cases goes to their cosigners. In turn, individuals would no longer have student debt hanging over their heads, and would be free to pursue whatever career path they please regardless of future earnings potential. They might even be able to buy a house. Don't get too excited as there is lots more to learn.

Don't you think that the current poorer performing colleges should be required to better analyze and advertise their graduation rates, earnings potential by major, and student debt statistics? They cannot simply suggest that it is great being here, throw down $100,000 and risk losing it all because of our incompetence.

How about legislating that universities create offices of financial literacy to create a direct link between students and their loans? Financial literacy officers would be able to make it clear to students how to pay their loans, amounts, interest on the debt, and length of time they could be paying back their loans. If after year one, depending on the prospects for students with such a class rank, the student should be advised to withdraw and save a ton of money in the future.

Mitch Daniels for all I have seen wants to solve this problem the best way. He has created an office similar to this at Purdue, and he was able to lower student loan defaults to the low single-digits across campus. In addition, before students even choose a college, the FAFSA needs to be simplified, in order for students to more easily qualify for student aid.

College is meant to be as accessible and affordable for everyone as functionally possible, but it should not encourage anybody to go into debt when their future prospects for a job and repayment are grim.

All facts should be disseminated in the media to which the student is most comfortable. Parents must also be informed, especially if they are forced to cosign. Actually, I would lift the cosign requirement and instead insist the university kick junior out of he is not in the top half of his class.

Lastly for some but firstly for me, colleges must have major skin in the game. Whether through incentives or punishment, universities need to pay for poor default and loan repayment rates. They can pay initial penalties via their massive endowments but after that, they need to be put out of the student loan or ISA business if their product is not usable in America.

Through federal or state governments, funding incentives could also be created for schools that make year over year improvements to their default and repayment rates.

On the other hand, schools could be forced to pay a small portion of student loan payments in years that their default/non-repayment are exceptionally high, in order to remain in the federal program. These incentives would help universities have a reason for concern about their students' success and ability to pay back their loans.

Chapter Conclusion

By understanding the roles of all the involved parties, one can consider ways in which each role can be better fit or incentivized to help make the system work better for all. Through some simple fixes (shortened FAFSA), and others more complex (federal government ISA program), efforts can be made to simplify and create opportunity for students, private entities, educational institutions, and the US Government. In all of these situations, the American College Student needs to be at the top of the consideration list.

Overall, one cannot emphasize enough the importance of this issue. Government student loan debt has tripled in the past ten years, and without making any changes, it will not be getting better.

It is very uncertain what debt levels will be another decade from now. With more and more positions requiring degrees, the best thing America can do for its constituents is to offer simple, affordable, quality postsecondary education. Perhaps corporations should develop standardized essay and comprehensive examinations that can serve as markers in addition to GPAs for students willing to take such exams.

Most importantly though, the cost of education must be manageable and shared by more than just individual students and the American taxpayers. Through creating valuable synergies between students, educational institutions, the private sector, and the government, a much more efficient system can be implemented. Amen on that!

While students are ultimately responsible; it is also America's constitutional responsibility to create opportunity for its citizens—just like public schools exist for K-12.

I would encourage you to reflect on all those you know that are affected by student debt. This may be friends, family, yourself, or even your favorite barista at the local Starbucks down the street – all of whom are struggling to mitigate sometimes-unmanageable student loans.

Each individual may have a different story, but all have debt in common. Something that affects seven out of ten Americans should, and will soon be, a top priority or there will be a lot of ***former*** Congresspersons.

As John Harvey of Forbes asserts, "Of course, one could rightly argue that no one forced them to go to college. They freely chose to extend their education beyond high-school leaving age and take on all this debt. But, it isn't as if they are taking out these loans to buy big-screen TVs or take Caribbean cruises.

Moreover, at sixteen, seventeen, and eighteen years of age, these students are so positive on life, just as the smoking, the drug, and the credit card hustlers are getting them early, it is unfortunate but true that the marketing hustlers in our finest universities are convincing them to give up the debt for the greater life and the pleasure of enjoying their university. They never talk about the reality of repayment after graduation.

If I had it my way, I would forgive all student loans immediately, those who can pay and those who cannot, and I know the economy would boom. I bet the economic upturn would pay for itself. Everybody would be happy, and the US would learn a big lesson about loaning dollars to any student less than 21-years of age.

It I understandable that students invest in themselves. In a world, were participation trophies are awarded rather than permitting competition. Students start out not really knowing how good they are. Life is fairer when it is honestly fair. Students who engage in loans to get ahead are trying to increase what economists call human capital. They want to acquire new skills, learn new ways of thinking, and to develop specializations in particular areas of study. In short, they want to better themselves. Some at 17 or 18 years of age are simply not ready, just like they are not ready to be permitted to consume a case of beer on a Friday night.

And, when students finish school and get a great job, we all gain. Nothing resounds truer than this idea. College education benefits more than just the student. It benefits more than the receiver of tuition, textbook manufacturers, loan servicers, or luxury off-campus housing complexes. When American citizens receive a college education, it benefits us all.

But, when it costs these impressionable people (millennials) their future, they realize they should have been taught better in college—but were not because their professors had a coffee-breath ideological bent. The lifetime earnings of so many people, mostly the young and vulnerable have been disrupted because the whole deal was and continues to be a fraud! But, we are America and we Americans own the Congress and we therefore own a means of making it all better.

✓

Chapter 15 A Debt Plan for Student Debtors

Should students take on all the risk?

Sam Clovis was the national co-chair and policy director of Trump's campaign. He has presented a number of Trump ideas that are still a work-in-progress. Few things regarding student loan debt are final as this matter in the Trump Administration and this topic is too important to rush.

Before the election in 2016, Clovis spoke about Student Debt Issues on behalf of candidate Trump. The Trump campaign expected that higher education was to be a major issue in the fall general election. He was 100% right and Trump had the right ideas. Trump knows there are some good ways to solve the debt crisis and we have already discussed many of them in this book.

[A number of the notions in this chapter have come from the web site-- insidehighered.com.]

Colleges & Universities share the loan risk

One proposal being prepared sounds especially appealing. It would alter the current system of student loans in which students have all the risk. It would force all colleges to share the risk of such loans and make it harder for those wanting to major in the liberal arts at non-elite institutions to obtain guaranteed loans. Statistics show that the latter are less likely to be able to pay off a student loan as their incomes if they can get jobs would be quite low. This is a groundbreaking notion.

Trump is well aware that a number of his ideas might face a skeptical Congress. Nonetheless his ideas have gained considerable attention.

One simply must ask if Congress is so smart in evaluating proposals: "Why has it not solved the problem?"

From a parent's perspective, Congress is the greatest enemy of parents caught in the student loan mess. It was Congress that created the law that even students with no means of paying back a loan—those who are in fact bankrupt, still must carry that loan on their backs until the day the student loan holder dies.

Mr. Clovis is a tenured professor of economics at Morningside College, a small private college in Iowa. He took a leave of absence to help the Trump campaign.

Some of Clovis' recent pronouncements on Trump policies have been widely criticized by the same Washington experts and bureaucrats who had been advising President Obama. They find Trump's work as unworkable or unrealistic. Yet, their record is one of complete failure for eight long years.

Clovis said he expected some higher education leaders to react the same way as Trump outlined these ideas in the recently successful campaign. From the beginning, Clovis noted, the campaign remained open to ideas as long as they put the emphasis on student success in ways that have more impact than the failed efforts of past administrations.

Clovis said. "How do you pay for that? It's absurd on its surface." Trump has ideas to pay for everything, including the massive student debt load.

Further, Trump also rejects President Obama's proposals for a state-federal partnership to make community college free for new high school graduates. Community colleges are "damn near free" now, and "almost anyone can afford community college," he said. It is funny that Obama and Hillary are teaming up again on solutions for problems that have been here for each of the past eight years. Where were their solutions when they were in control?

Big Changes for Student Loans

The Trump campaign and now the Trump Administration is working on a complete overhaul of the federal student loan system. Few Americans felt comfortable when Obama got rid of Sallie Mae and then began to make over $40 billion a year on the backs of former students.

Trump is moving the government out of lending and restoring that role to private banks, and places like Sallie Mae. This was how things were before President Clinton partially and President Obama fully shifted loan origination from private lenders to the government. What does government do well? Not much!

"We think it should be marketplace and market driven," he said. Local banks should be lending to local students, he said, but colleges should be playing a role in determining loan worthiness on factors that go beyond family income.

Further, Clovis said that all colleges should have "skin in the game" and share the risk associated with student loans. Many in Congress (and not just Republicans) have voiced support for that idea.

Unfortunately, Democrats are looking to get some favors for their constituencies, which seem to be the foreign nationals on student visas. The forgotten American is still not remembered by Democrats. The Democrats are arguing already that some institutions -- historically black colleges, for example -- should be exempt, given their histories of educating many students from low-income families who may not have the financial resources of others. But Clovis said that the principle of colleges sharing risk must apply to all institutions.

Further, the overall plans in this book, recognize that the risk needs to be substantial enough to change the way colleges decide whether to admit students, and which programs they offer. After being promised the sun and the moon by admissions counsellors for years, many students fortunate enough to graduate, not only cannot get a job, they have massive debt and they have no means to pay it.

Clovis said he hoped many colleges would continue to provide remediation for those unprepared for college-level work, although he said that he preferred the term "student success programs" to remediation.

He noted that colleges should not be admitting students that they aren't confident can graduate in a reasonable time frame and find jobs. There is little sense for somebody who is a high risk of not finishing college to become engrossed in debt.

Therefore, those who decide who gets student loans, when looking at those students with less emphasis on parent contributions and the Free Application for Federal Student Aid, need to consider more of "a partnership" between the student, the bank and the college. "We think if the college has real skin in the game, it will change its model."

And these reforms would make it legitimate for colleges and banks to make decisions in part on students' prospective majors and their likely earnings after graduation, he said.

"If you are going to study 16th-century French art, more power to you. I support the arts," Clovis said. "But you are not going to get a job."

A college should factor that in when deciding on a student's loan eligibility, and the requirement that colleges share the risk would be a powerful incentive to do so, Clovis added. Ya gotta love an educator such as Clovis getting in front of this issue so well.

"If you get into the esoteric aspects of a particular art field, you have to know that those are the circumstances," he said. The moral of the story is that "colleges may not get a new student if they tell the student the truth and they prevent likely defaulters from getting loans. So, they give up something while a prospective student gets a way to figure out how to move ahead without such heavy lifelong loan drag."

Clovis presents the fact that Trump is not against the liberal arts. The fact is that liberal arts positions are few and far between and in most cases, and they pay less than the hard sciences. "The liberal arts education is the absolute foundation to success in life," Clovis said, adding that he hoped business and engineering and health professions and education students would include liberal arts courses in their college educations.

But it is a different thing altogether, Clovis said, to focus on such fields. "If you choose to major in the liberal arts, there are issues associated with that." Not ever getting a job in your field, and becoming a bartender are two of the issues.

There may be colleges that decide they would be happy backing loans for students who study the liberal arts. That gives college's more skin in the game if they think their education is worth the risk. A prestigious college could legitimately decide that anyone it graduates -- regardless of major -- will do well in life, and so go ahead with approving the borrowing.

"If you go to Harvard, you can major in anything you want, and once you get in the door, you'll be OK," Clovis said, so such a college might be fine with its students borrowing to study the liberal arts. "But not all colleges are in the same system," he said.

Community Colleges, For-Profits and More

The Trump campaign would encourage community colleges, in much the same fashion as four-year colleges, to focus on serving students who can succeed. Helping students succeed is also a worthwhile effort but minimizing risk in the loan area is paramount for both the student and the institution.

Based on his research, Clovis said, there is much for community colleges to be proud of. They do a great job in job-training programs for examples as well as preparing students for year three and four, of a four-year degree.

For-Profits need to be studied further according to Clovis. "The business model for for-profit higher education is quite different" from that of nonprofit colleges. The Trump administration is working to figure out how to propose improvements for the for-profit education sector.

The Obama administration had been widely seen as being very tough on the sector, and many Republicans in Congress had accused the prior administration of overstepping its authority in this area. Clovis, given a chance to weigh in on such criticism, chose to pass. He said the focus of the Trump campaign's and administration's ideas on higher education was public and private nonprofit higher education.

Trump's advisor is a fan of nonprofit colleges that adopt some strategies from for-profit models. For example, he praised Regis University, where he once taught. The institution has a traditional residential campus in Colorado, but a much larger student body enrolled online.

Remove the Department of Education.

Ron Paul and Donald Trump both want the Department of Education to be eliminated. "Once we get into office, we're going to take a hard look at the Department of Education," Clovis said. "There are lots of things that serve people well, but there are many operations that do not.

In wrapping up his discussion, Clovis noted that
College administrators should be speaking out in defense of free speech, he said. "We need leadership that says that one side does not get to dictate what is said." Donald Trump is a free speech advocate. Many campuses had shut down all free speech related to the Trump Presidential campaign. What a shame.

There is no question that Trump's plan can help the Student debt issue in two ways. 1. By helping those with minimal chances of success in college to avoid the massive life-ruining debt of massive student loans. 2. Paying off the loan debt through a number of clever techniques, and permitting students to be removed from default when they pay anything.

The problem is real, and Trump is ready to solve it. I am counting on him reading this book to gain additional ideas or solidify those he already is contemplating.

It is definitely not a myth. A friend of mine's son just completed his Masters in sociology at a private four-year institution where he also obtained his BA. His total education debt is now almost $190,000. His best job offer is for $27,000.

He would have done as well or better with a teaching certificate. Students and their parents really do need to look at the probable jobs and salaries of their chosen field before taking on that kind of debt.

God bless all the students who do the right thing to protect their futures in a forward way and who protect their futures by not ensnaring themselves in exorbitant debt.

Thank you for giving a few page-turns in this book. Please send the President a book and I will reimburse you for sure. Your picture will be in the next edition.

God bless America!

Other books by Brian Kelly: (amazon.com, and Kindle)

Boost Social Security Now! Hey Buddy Can You Spare a Dime?
The Birth of American Football. From the first college game in 1869 to the last Super Bowl
Obamacare: A One-Line Repeal Congress must get this done.
A Wilkes-Barre Christmas Story A wonderful town makes Christmas all the better
A Boy, A Bike, A Train, and a Christmas Miracle A Christmas story that will melt your heart
Pay-to-Go America-First Immigration Fix
Legalizing Illegal Aliens Via Resident Visas Americans-first plan saves $Trillions. Learn how!
60 Million Illegal Aliens in America!!! A simple, America-first solution.
The Bill of Rights By Founder James Madison Refresh *your knowledge of the specific rights for all*
Great Players in Army Football Great Army Football played by great players..
Great Coaches in Army Football Army's coaches are all great.
Great Moments in Army Football Army Football at its best.
Great Moments in Florida Gators Football Gators Football from the start. This is the book.
Great Moments in Clemson Football CU Football at its best. This is the book.
Great Moments in Florida Gators Football Gators Football from the start. This is the book.
The Constitution Companion. A Guide to Reading and Comprehending the Constitution
The Constitution by Hamilton, Jefferson, & Madison – Big type and in English
PATERNO: The Dark Days After Win # 409. Sky began to fall within days of win # 409.
JoePa 409 Victories: Say No More! Winningest Division I-A football coach ever
American College Football: The Beginning From before day one football was played.
Great Coaches in Alabama Football Challenging the coaches of every other program!
Great Coaches in Penn State Football the Best Coaches in PSU's football program
Great Players in Penn State Football The best players in PSU's football program
Great Players in Notre Dame Football The best players in ND's football program
Great Coaches in Notre Dame Football The best coaches in any football program
Great Players in Alabama Football from Quarterbacks to offensive Linemen Greats!
Great Moments in Alabama Football AU Football from the start. This is the book.
Great Moments in Penn State Football PSU Football, start--games, coaches, players,
Great Moments in Notre Dame Football ND Football, start, games, coaches, players
Cross Country With the Parents A great trip from East Coast to West with the kids
Seniors, Social Security & the Minimum Wage. Things seniors need to know.
How to Write Your First Book and Publish It with CreateSpace
The US Immigration Fix--It's all in here. Finally, an answer.
I had a Dream IBM Could be #1 Again The title is self-explanatory
WineDiets.Com Presents The Wine Diet Learn how to lose weight while having fun.
Wilkes-Barre, PA; Return to Glory Wilkes-Barre City's return to glory
Geoffrey Parsons' Epoch... The Land of Fair Play Better than the original.
The Bill of Rights 4 Dummmies! This is the best book to learn about your rights.
Sol Bloom's Epoch ...Story of the Constitution The best book to learn the Constitution
America 4 Dummmies! All Americans should read to learn about this great country.
The Electoral College 4 Dummmies! How does it really work?
The All-Everything Machine Story about IBM's finest computer server.
ThankYou IBM! This book explains how IBM was beaten in the computer marketplace by neophytes

Brian has written over 300 books in total. Other books can be found at amazon.com/author/brianwkelly

www.ingramcontent.com/pod-product-compliance
Lightning Source LLC
LaVergne TN
LVHW051838080426
835512LV00018B/2942